PRASE FOR B

"Greg's unique history of rebuilding trust, carving new paths to unite uncommon neighbors, and leading an innovative work that demonstrates what restoration looks like when we get to the end of ourselves makes this a must read for anyone called to work for cultural renewal." —**Gabe Lyons**, author of The Next Christians and founder of Q

"I love Greg Fromholz. He's a genius at forging subversive friend-ships among unlikely friends. And that is because people trust him. This book is his about how to restore trust. It's a cookbook for collaboration, where Greg unveils some of his secret recipes for how we can restore trust in a fragmented world. Greg knows that we can do more good together than we can do on our own, and he has taken on the task of helping build a movement whose sole mission is to conspire together to redeem the world and to plot goodness all over the planet." —**Shane Claiborne**, author and activist, RedLetter Christians.org

"It is fitting that Greg has chosen trust as the central theme of this wonderful new book. Fitting because we have come to implicitly trust his voice as a poet, his vision as a prophet, and his heart as a pastor. Broken is yet another great example of the ease with which Greg blends his simultaneous callings as artist, pastor, and story-teller to be a blessing to the church. In a world (and sadly a church) in which we experience the sting of betrayal and disloyalty all too often, we can trust Greg to lead us on the journey to renewed hope in our trustworthy Savior." —**Chris Llewellyn**, Rend Collective

"In Broken, Greg Fromholz focuses on the essential but scary ingredient of peace building: TRUST. Trust is the real peacemaker's challenge that won't be satisfied with a placard or bumper sticker. He chooses the most untrusting of opponents—the Sacred and the Sec-ular—opting not just to talk of 'building trust' or 'maintaining trust' but to confront the enormous problem of 'restoring trust' when trust has been lost. His slingshot arguments laced with self-deprecating humor are typical Fromholz. I'm happy to endorse this book." —**Jack Heaslip**, late spiritual advisor to U2

"Greg Fromholz is one of the most gifted, inspired, and articulate leaders in the Euro-American Church today. Here, in an appealing but very direct pastiche of autobiographical stories and professional observations, he calls us to the central and compelling mission of the Church. That is, as his subtitle suggests, he calls us to the business, imperative in our time, of restoring trust between the sacred and the secular." —**Phyllis Tickle**, author of *Emergence Christianity*

"Greg takes us through fear and beyond by a potent combination of literary expressions: autobiography, modern parable, and Holy Scripture. His theme is that of restoring trust in hard places by going into the whirlwind of fear and being accompanied through this maelstrom by The Other and by God. His skill as a communicator shines through in the written word, which at times is as close to poetry as it is to prose. He is clear that communication is service of the Word of God. A number of compelling themes for our time cause us to stop, pray, and think afresh, for example: compassion precedes justice, and collaboration is the catalyst for change. This book is perspective-changing. Please read it." —**The Most Reverend Dr. Jackson**, Archbishop of Dublin and Bishop of Glendalough

"Most Irishmen head for America. Greg Fromholz has returned the favor. He's an iconoclast who likes tradition, an innovator with a passion for reconciliation, a broken healer, a sinner who can't help but be a saint. When Greg makes films, I watch them. When he talks I listen—with an accent like that you can't not. When Greg writes books I read them. And when he writes a book about the world made whole, I want everyone to take note." —**Pete Greig**, 24-7 Prayer, Emmaus Road

"Greg is the real deal. Always committed to bringing people together across all walks of life. Not just a good man but a great man, happy to be in the shadows but able to lead an army." —**Martin Smith**, artist, writer, producer, former member of Delirious?, MartinSmith.tv

"Greg Fromholz has to be one of the leading Christian leaders of our age. His personality exudes a passion for ministry to young adults. His ability to connect with people is enviable and inspiring. His ministry emanates from a heart that is immersed in the Christian message of love and hope. Through his work he empowers young adults to be effective leaders in the community of faith to which they belong. Greg's message crosses all boundaries of faith tradition, culture, and ethnicity. His enthusiasm for empowering young adults is infectious, and he is rightly known as a key leader in developing church for the modern age." —**The Very Reverend Dermot Dunne**, Dean of Christ Church Cathedral

"To paraphrase Vanilla Ice, Broken invites us to stop, listen, and collaborate. In his inimitable way, Gregory Fromholz puts flesh on what too often feels like the dry bones of scripture and its denizens. We hear and believe the living word of God when it's on the lips of our trusted cultural interpreter—the author—a humble explorer on the trails of this world (and the one to come) who asks us to walk with him. Pack your rucksack and courage, leave fear behind, and join the journey to openhearted redemption." —**Cathleen Falsani**, author of The God Factor and Sin Boldly

PRAISE FOR
LIBERATE EDEN

"In my travels, I'm amazed in country after country to meet leaders with extraordinary creativity and spiritual sensitivity, seeking to articulate the heart of their faith in language that feels authentic to them and that will communicate to their peers as well. In Ireland, Greg Fromholz is one such leading voice." —**Brian McLaren**, author and activist, BrianMcLaren.net

"This book is a work of art, and like any work of art it draws us into intimate communion with the artist. Greg Fromholz carries us through the turmoil of the heart and mind that all people of faith must travel. He brings us up and out of the dark tower that we must climb if we are to bask in the light of God's glory. I give this book two thumbs up!" —**Tony Campolo**, professor emeritus at Eastern University, St. David's, Pennsylvania

"Greg Fromholz is a man deeply rooted in Christian faith and belonging, who is prepared to live close to the edge of his inherited Christian culture and to hear and engage with the angst and searching of those for whom faith seems utterly foreign and irrelevant. I have been both encouraged and challenged by the manner in which Greg shares and lives a dynamic Christian faith." —**The Right Reverend Dr. John Neill**, Primate of Ireland and Metropolitan and former Archbishop of Dublin and Bishop of Glendalough

"Greg Fromholz is unafraid of exploration. He shows a daring, a cheekiness, a presumption that would delight a loving parent. He tackles God, the world, religion, himself with an energy that is healthily uncomfortable and often shocking. He reveals a passion for worship—employing all the senses to celebrate creativity with imagination, drama, and fun. He issues an invitation to us to magnify the Lord with him." —**Jack Heaslip**, late spiritual advisor to U2

"Words almost never fail me, and they haven't failed me in my struggle to capture here the essence of Liberate Eden. Rather, the problem is that I have too many words from which to choose, words like as poignant, graphic, stark, and luxuriant as any book I have seen in years . . . or simultaneously convicting and salvific . . . or full of grace, beauty, and a frankness that knows no measure and is without relief . . . or a labyrinth of compelling juxtapositions. Perhaps, better said, given this wealth of possibilities, is that this book is a journey worth taking." —**Phyllis Tickle**, author of *Emergence Christianity*

"Listen to this fellow. Greg's plugged into the Source. He's listening carefully—to his own life and the life of the Spirit. Liberate Eden is a major breath of fresh air for the church and a huge blessing to me personally." —**Cathleen Falsani**, journalist and author

"As a band who hold on to the old-fashioned beliefs of commitment to relationships, we are drawn to people of integrity and heart. Greg Fromholz is one such chap. He is not just an author, dreamer, and seeker but a man who also treasures people. He is a believer that as the church lays down its comforts and picks up its cross, the future will be bright and the world, hope infused." —**Rend Collective**

BROKEN

restoring trust between
the sacred & the secular

GREG FROMHOLZ

ABINGDON PRESS | NASHVILLE

Broken: Restoring Trust Between the Sacred and the Secular
Copyright © 2015 by Gregory Fromholz

Macro Editor: Lauren Winner
Published in association with Christopher Ferebee Literary Agency.
Library of Congress Cataloging-in-Publication Data
Fromholz, Greg.
  Broken : restoring trust between the sacred and the secular / Greg Fromholz.
    pages cm
  Includes bibliographical references.
  ISBN 978-1-4267-9635-7 (binding: soft back) 1. Christianity and culture. 2. Christianity—Influence. 3. Christian life. 4. Trust—Religious aspects—Christianity. I. Title.
  BR115.C8F75 2015
  261—dc23

                                                          2015023234

Excerpts have been reprinted from the author's Book App "Liberate Eden" (Matthew and Owen: 2011).

15 16 17 18 19 20 21 22 23 24—10 9 8 7 6 5 4 3 2 1
MANUFACTURED IN THE UNITED STATES OF AMERICA

Thanks

For my wonderful family Alex, Chlöe, Joshua, and Eden

. . . and for all who crave hope.

Special thanks to Alexandra Fromholz, Jack Heaslip, Chris Ferebee, Pádraig Ó Tuama, Anna Moran, John Ryan, Joseph von Meding, Peter Neill, Paul Carroll, Rob and Dilys Jones, Eoin Wright, Roly Miller, Scott Evans, Gareth and Ali Gilkeson

Additional thanks to Bob and Sonya, Jeff, Mom, Chris and Gabby, Patrick, Dad and Char, Eo and Becky, Rob, Shane, Phyllis, Brian, Cathleen, Foy, Pete, Don, Jim, Cameron and Katy, Mary B., Gemma, Roberta, Derek, Eanna, Jasper, Dermot, Stan, John and Sue, Sandy and Carina, Terry and Sheila, David, Martin, Tim, Basil, Ger, Paul C., Q and Cathy, Lisa, Susie and Paul, Niall, Jude, Toby, Paul R., Dave and Emily, Aaron and Corrie, Scott and Zoe

Contents

Introduction xi

1. Trust and Forgiveness: The Addict, the Artist, the
   Father, and His Son 1

2. Trust and Separation: The Embrace of "Nothings" 14

3. Trust and Presence: Strangling My Inner Jesus . . . 30

4. Trust and Fear: The Day Everything Changed 46

5. Trust and Posture: Living with Change 56

6. Trust and Restoration: The Shattering
   of Misrepresentation 72

7. Trust and Faithfulness: Who Me? 89

8. Trust and Freedom: I Can See Clearly Now 104

9. Trust and Being: We, the Church 119

10. Trust and Peace: The Abnormality of Beauty 130

11. Trust and Hope: Embracing Our True Selves 142

12. Trust and Scars: A Life of Broken Restoration . . . 154

13. Trust and Honor: The Radical Solidarity
    of Service 166

14. Trust and Home: The Sound of Crashing Tables
    in Sacred Spaces 179

15. Trust and Living: All Our Beautiful Castles 193

16. Trust and Collaboration: Seek the Common. . . . 207

Notes 223

Introduction

The greatest need in society today is trust. I want to trust more. We want to trust more. But there's a lot that gets in the way.

The places we thought we could trust the most have done a stellar job of letting us down and not easily; like the partner who just turned up to *our* date with a new date, no warning, just a different lover. Distrust grows in the soil of betrayal. I know that *betrayal* seems like a dramatic word, but to trust in someone or something, to invest, to hold close to your chest and to allow the other to enter into a loyalty is a beautiful thing to behold; for this to turn on you can feel dramatic . . . because it is dramatic.

We can list our betrayals as easily as writing a grocery list; fathers, mothers, brothers and sisters, girlfriends, boy-friends, banks, churches, media, the police, government, God; the list goes on—broken trust is as individual as the thoughts we carry in the dark and as ubiquitous as neon in Vegas.

The unfortunate equation to follow would be something like: humans = distrust. And our lives and institutions are absolutely filled with us, humanity.

We have been let down by institutions, let down by ourselves. It used to be safe to save, safe to pray, safe to love, safe to get information from the media, easier to see justice—but true justice leaves no one behind, and there are now many left behind.

Broken promises have severed trust with our money, our faith, our creativity, our justice, our lives. Distrust is now our collective scar—personally and institutionally, sacred and secular.

Yet we still cash checks, believe beyond ourselves, watch TV, obey the law, and love. Why? Because we need to—want to—trust again. It is our greatest need; and it's an innate, instinctive desire, even deeper than desire.

It doesn't matter who you are or where you're from—we've all experienced distrust, and we all desire to trust one another again. Trust trumps everything. Can we love, hope, have faith, or forgive without trust? Traction for living is found in the depth of trust.

How do we start restoring trust in our lives and communities? We start where trust is found most readily: in our shared experiences, in our commonality, in our very lives.[1]

I feel like this book could've been titled many things: *Jesus Failed: Or Have We?* or *Connect. Create. Collaborate: Rediscovering the Art of Trust* or *It's All About the Enchiladas* (this will make more sense later); but we went with *Broken* because it recognizes, without fear, the reality of the state of trust that exists in faith today. This book is an attempt to excavate and scrutinize that broken trust with a faith that shows how that which is wounded can be healed and that which is broken can be restored.

One

Trust and Forgiveness

The Addict, the Artist, the Father, and His Son

WARPED POLAROIDS

"I'm not comfortable in my own skin. I don't think I was made for this earth." I had been playing Frisbee with this ghost from my past for nearly two hours now in the front parking lot of a home for Alzheimer's patients. This was my temporary home, and for my biological father, it seems earth was his. I met him for the first time in my living memory at the age of eighteen. Up until then, I could only remember him from warped Polaroids of a lost childhood. Since then, my father had become a friend, though he would never really be a father. Trust offered is not a trust restored—there is an active ingredient, a conduit, an accelerant for trust to be restored, and that is forgiveness.

If relationship is the key that unlocks trust's home, then forgiveness must be the permanent guest. But forgiveness is a slippery grasp and can be extremely elusive, especially when you need it.

My elusive, Frisbee-throwing father was named Dan.

He was six feet seven inches tall.

He was the son of a man who survived the World War II
Normandy invasion, a soldier who tragically died
of alcoholism.

He was a musician.

He was a poet.

He was a peace activist during the Vietnam War.

He wore a necklace of a peace sign over his Coast Guard
dress whites.

He marched against Nixon in Chicago.

He was an environmentalist in the 1960s and '70s,
before it was cool to be green.

He had a marijuana "plantation" in his basement.

He was married three times.

He was divorced three times.

He was diagnosed with schizophrenia at the age of 21.

He was put on experimental cocktails of drugs to give him
"balance."

He was an alcoholic, like his father and grandfather
before him.

He had two dogs, Dylan and Bojangles.

He liked to garden naked.

We share many traits in life; many that I'm thankful for
and a few that I could've done without.

Eighteen years after my birth, Dan was at the airport, and
no one had told me he was coming.

I had been living overseas and was coming back for a
quick visit. The airport was crowded as I collected my lug-
gage and exited into the arrivals hall. A nerve-ridden, quick

scan left and right, in case my family had forgotten to collect me, revealed that I couldn't have been more wrong. My whole family had turned up: aunts, uncles, cousins, brothers, mother, grandmother, and a very tall guy in the back—like Big Bird without the feathers.

You know that moment when you've walked past a person on the street or turned up to a party and that person across from you is very familiar but you just can't place him or her? As I approached and got all the wonderfully missed hugs that only family can give, I kept catching the eye of this giant bystander. Was this my dad? In many ways it was easier to call him Dan than Dad; one consonant makes a lot of difference with it comes to inconsistency of relationship. But did anyone at any point think it would've been a good idea to tell me he was coming? "By the way, Greg, your long-lost father is gonna pop by and say 'Hi'." (No wonder I have trust issues.)

As the hugs died down, I looked up and walked toward my dad. My insides were like a lonely shoe in the spin cycle of a tumble dryer: I was convinced that everyone around me could hear the erratic thumps of my soul. Everything was in slow motion. So many choices were cascading onto my melting brain.

The most physical, emotional, and spiritual thing a human being can do is choose. Everything begins with a choice. And it was time to make mine. Would I just walk past him and ignore him the way he did me for most of my life? Would I walk straight up to him and shout a long line of expletives, spit flying from my hurt and enraged lips? Would I grab a ladder, climb up it, and punch him in the face?

All were justifiable responses, I think, in the present circumstance. The question would be not *which one* I would choose but *which order* I would unleash them in. He was guilty of walking away, there was no doubt, and I wanted to draw a crowd of accusers and bring a swift bit of justice to the scene. Where are stones to be found in this sterile airport arrivals hall?

But something very odd happened; a light bulb in the recesses of my soul flickered and caught my attention. God was at work igniting that filament. God was getting between Dan and me. An idea not of my own landed like a punch line—*Greg, you need to forgive him.*

I wanted to pull my ribs apart and shout, *What? Are you insane? God, I know you've seen all this unfold before you, but he doesn't deserve to walk back into my life and get forgiveness, get trust, get a relationship.* Again the flickering, the understanding speaks, *Greg, you need to forgive him.* God wanted to "pull my ribs apart and let the sun inside."[1]

I had been attempting—and failing at the attempt—to live a life of faith for a number of years at this point, and I knew in this moment that even if I couldn't trust myself, my biological father, or even the ever-splitting churches we were part of, that deep down, this was a moment to trust the Creator.

I walked up to Dan, looked him in the eyes, and embraced him, saying only five words twice, "It's going to be OK. It's going to be OK." The orchestrated soundtrack music didn't swell, and we didn't cut to a montage of us playing ball on the beach with the sun setting, but we did begin a future right there in the arrivals hall.

New trust brings new futures.

The most physical, emotional, and spiritual thing a human being can do is choose. Everything begins with a choice. And this had been a tough one.

But in the embrace, a lightness came over my whole body, and a weight, which I had gotten so good at carrying that I didn't even realize it was present, was now dissipating.

A restorative path was set by the indiscriminate act of giving a second chance.

In the car as we drove away, my younger brother leaned over and said, "I guess no one told you Dan was coming." Squeezing my hand, he added, "It's going to be OK."

Sometimes forgiveness needs to surprise us. Sometimes trust is established when you least expect it. But it takes willingness in the moment and the intention to work it out beyond the scene unfolding—a willingness that comes from deep within. This is connection. This is restoration. This is redemption. This is trust reestablished. And this is God's passion for humanity.

OCEANS OF JUSTICE

> The religion scholars and Pharisees led in a woman who had been caught in an act of adultery. They stood her in plain sight of everyone and said, "Teacher, this woman was caught red-handed in the act of adultery. Moses, in the Law, gives orders to stone such persons. What do you say?" . . .
> Jesus bent down and wrote with his finger in the dirt. (John 8:3-8 *The Message*)

As the stone falls from my hand, I can't help but feel a release. My hand had become numb from clutching it so hard; I had grown used to the accuser's weapon. Was it regret or revelation that released the projectile from my grip to the ground? Sometimes they feel like the same thing. I would have been one of the last to leave, mesmerized by the bravery infused with kindness in his eyes as he knelt before that shaking woman.

Jesus was unafraid to keep the law of the land while simultaneously bending it into new forms. Swords into ploughshares, AK47s into garden tools.[2] Back in the day, sins were scribbled in the dust of the temple floors. Back in the day, names of sinners were scribbled next to them. We may scoff at this now, thinking how barbaric. But what lasts longer: the sins and the sinner's name written in dust or those written in the accuser's heart? To write is to remember, but writing in the dirt implies impermanence. This was the Jesus way. When it came to sin, Jesus was all about the washable Crayola markers, the permanent Sharpies broken in two.

> They continued to question him, so he stood up and replied, "Whoever hasn't sinned should throw the first stone." Bending down again, he wrote on the ground. (John 8:7-8)

The Creator's hands in the dirt, again.

Did Jesus write the names of the accusers? Did Jesus write the names of sinners and their sins? Or did he just draw a line, daring the accusers to take one more step?

> Those who heard him went away, one by one, beginning with the elders. Finally, only Jesus and

the woman were left in the middle of the crowd.
(John 8:9)

Jesus stands, Jesus sits, Jesus reaches, Jesus touches. Jesus' posture is not arrogant. His knees are dirty. His reach is not patronizing.

Jesus' love is *with* not *at*. Jesus is there in the dirt, in the woman's brokenness, in solidarity with her. Jesus puts himself firmly between the accuser and the accused. The incarnate God now a human shield.

WOULD YOU LIKE FRIES WITH THAT?

I was happily sipping my chocolate shake after a good night out with friends. The table across from us on the left held a fifty-something couple. The table across from us on the right held a couple in their late teens.

Two a.m. "What the hell did you call me?" broke the early morning's calm. The young girl was livid. "You're a little slut!" shot from the mouth of the fifty-something woman.

I have no idea what could've caused this commotion, but the usually buzzing fast-food restaurant was frozen, all eyes on our neighboring booths. It escalated quickly with the young boyfriend shouting at the fifty-somethings and the fifty-somethings retaliating with throwing a strawberry milkshake onto the young girl. The young boyfriend wasted no time in diving across the table, meeting the fifty-something man in the middle. The woman and girl dove in too. Yet the patrons stood frozen, eyes wide. I'm not sure how I got from behind my booth in time, but there I was, arms spread wide trying to break up an escalating situation and now covered in strawberry milkshake and looking for anyone to break from their catatonic state and help out. No one did. I looked at the fifty-somethings and said, "What are you doing? You should know better!" The fifty-somethings shot back with milkshake-colored language and loads of excuses, "He said . . . she said." But I didn't care. I just looked at them and said, "You should know better. It doesn't matter what was said. You're supposed to know better." I then reached down and drew a line in the sticky shake on the linoleum floor, and they . . . No, I didn't do that, but wouldn't that have been cool? What I did do, though, was turn to the young, shaking girl, look her in the eyes, and say, "I don't care what you've done; you are not what they are calling you. You are so much better. It's going to be OK." She mouthed, with tear-filled eyes, "Thank you." Was she guilty? I don't know—I just knew she was in need. Compassion comes first. Compassion precedes justice.

The staff finally arrived. The fifty-somethings left mumbling. The young teenage couple cleaned themselves up, and I finished my chocolate shake, feeling awkward. And just as I exited, the whole of the fast-food joint woke from its slumber and broke into an after-school-special-type applause.

Yet Jesus never waited for applause. Forgiveness restores in silence. Forgiveness is shaped in the hearts of those bold enough to be unpopular.

APPLES

Without hesitation, Jesus places himself between the accuser and the accused. It's nonnegotiable.

When reading the Bible or observing life, I often ask my-self the question, *Where am I in this story? Where am I in the stories of the "I am"?*

When looking at the story of the accused woman, where do you find yourself?

Are you a bystander?
Are your arms crossed, judging the accuser?
Do you have a stone in your hand?
Are you afraid?
Are you stepping forward to defend?
Are you on the ground, hands covered in dirt, clothes torn?
Is your self-confidence hitting rock bottom?
Have all your shadows come to light?
Are you reaching out, or is someone reaching toward you?

I've always hated clichés, but one that I used as a mantra for decades was "I love the sinner but hate the sin." It seems so compassionate. So altruistic. But compassion laced with judgment is as prejudiced and as toxic as a poisoned apple.

Author, speaker, and social activist Tony Campolo says it best when commenting on this commonly held cliché.

> That's just the *opposite* of what Jesus says. Jesus never says, "Love the sinner but hate his sin," Jesus says, "Love the sinner and hate *your own* sin." And after you get rid of the sin in your own life, *then* you can begin talking about the sin in your brother or sister's life.[3]

We need to look at ourselves first.

I've tried. And no matter how hard I try, I cannot rid myself of sin. Only Jesus can do that, and though I am redeemed, that will have to wait until I've shed this skin. So maybe I should just shut up about other people's sins and get on to loving them where they are, where we are, together in the dirt, with Jesus.

Distrust thrives when we lack compassion.

HERESY

> Jesus stood up and said to her, "Woman, where are they? Is there no one to condemn you?"
> She said, "No one, sir." [No one.]
> Jesus said, "Neither do I condemn you. Go, and from now on, don't sin anymore." (John 8:10-11)

It felt like heresy.
It felt like crazy talk.
It felt like blasphemy.
It felt like freedom.
Amazing how one man's blasphemy is another woman's freedom.
Amazing how one person's blasphemy is another person's freedom.

The prophetic was alive before them. Words on pages revealed in skin and bones. Freedom had a name: Jesus. The "I am" before all of them.

How would I have responded to this grace? A truth had been spoken not so much in words but in a reverberating depth that was unexplainable. All of a sudden, that woman's fragmented self was feeling whole for the first time.

She was loved by love itself. This was a body-rattling revelation, and revelations lead to change. Grace is an active not a passive word.

Restoration brought through the indiscriminate act of giving a second chance.

What would I do there? I think I would either remain in the dirt on my knees weeping in disbelief or laugh like a madman set free in a mixture of joy and fear of what's next.

This was, is, grace revealed, exposed and gushing with no control mechanisms; for grace is a stallion wild and free. Grace is uncontrollable!

The unasked question was, *Would this revelation lead to change in her?* Would this kind of exposed grace change us? To the Pharisees and church rulers of the day, unanswered questions were a volatile virus. We, they, I, like control—especially when it comes to the eternal. It makes me feel as though I have a purpose, an entitled place where I can put my feet up and dole out the grace to those of my choosing. But control, never having been fully taken, had been thoroughly seized back—the control of God, a fiction, a fallacy of humanity. This revelation is the kind that "subverts violence and all those who depend on it for their security, affluence, and happiness."[4]

And before you know it, the career-religious are out of a job. Most likely saying to those around them, "Somebody better kill this guy before word gets out." Or mumbling, "I hope my boss doesn't hear about this."

LIP SERVICE

To the Pharisees and church rulers of the day, these were the times of the prophet Amos, from eight hundred years before, bursting through their opulently adorned temple floors, the permanent power structures revealing their temporary futilities.

We are in these times now.

Amos's time was a time when those who believed in God had devolved into a people of lip service; their sense of entitlement had eroded their relationship with God and with those in need, trust a long-forgotten construct. Justice was now blinded by the greed and arrogance of the chosen; their generational values now discarded in the gutters of history.

Amos spoke:

> I can't stand your religious meetings.
>   I'm fed up with your conferences and
>   conventions.
> I want nothing to do with your religion
>   projects,
>   your pretentious slogans and goals.
> I'm sick of your fund-raising schemes,
>   your public relations and image making.
> I've had all I can take of your noisy ego-music.
>   When was the last time you sang to me?
> Do you know what I want?
>   I want justice—oceans of it.
> I want fairness—rivers of it.
>   That's what I want. That's all I want.
> (Amos 5:21-24 The Message)

SIN AND STONES

The temptation in these times is to want to hide, hoping it will just get better, to turn and run from the fathers in the arrivals halls. But in these times we, as Christians and the church, seem to be known more for gathering with other stone throwers, waiting until it seems "safer" to leave, instead of engaging in the justice, asking for forgiveness and forgiving, doing whatever we can to reconnect.

In these times it would be so easy to place the church and the leaders of institutions that have dismantled trust in God's name, in God, on the firing line. But, annoyingly, if we look closely we will see Jesus in the very same dirt next to the very people I would throw stones at. A seemingly justified stone is still a stone.

We just can't become stone throwers who target the stone throwers—for *we* are *they*! Both the woman and her accusers needed forgiveness, restoration, and hope. Jesus offered all three. For no one is excluded from grace.

I want oceans of justice to wash away my sins and my stones. I want oceans of justice to bring a new tide of relationship to God and humanity. I want forgiveness and trust to wash in wide with every wave. And I so desperately want oceans of justice to bring hope back from the deep.

Yesterday is gone. Tomorrow has not yet come. We have only today. Let us begin.

—Mother Teresa

Two

Trust and Separation

The Embrace of "Nothings"

LOST

My mother does not have a moustache. She is not six feet five inches tall nor does she carry two six-packs of Budweiser in one hand while walking the fluorescent-lit cereal aisle of my childhood supermarket. To this day, I don't think she's ever been near any of the above, except the cereal aisle. But that didn't change the fact that as a young boy, I reached up and grabbed his hand thinking it was my mom's. The look of shock on both our faces was equal. I'm not sure who screamed the loudest or cried the most.

I've never really been lost, unless you count that fateful day in that mid-Michigan supermarket. But I've made plenty of wrong turns on my bike and in my car, once driving wide-eyed and terrified up the wrong way of a highway. Then there was the classic lostness that came when my friend Eric and I were waved to by a pretty blonde girl in a black Trans-Am with a T-shaped sunroof and a pair of gold, chain-link underwear hanging from her rearview mirror. She waved. We followed. She drove fast. We followed.

We ran out of gas. She did not. That was a long, embarrassing walk home.

I've never really been lost in the classic biblical sense of lost—the wandering in deserts for decades, the sheep wandering aimlessly across fields, the take-your-dad's-money-and-run kind of lost.

I've made plenty of wrong turns in life for sure and will continue to. I have experienced lostness on plenty of other levels and in plenty of other ways that feel biblical in size. I have severed trust and with that severing lost the warmth of being found. Yet in those times, I found myself embracing being lost far too comfortably. Warmth is warmth even if it's only temporary. But I soon realized that temporary is not living.

LOOK BACK

In Luke 15 we find one of the most popular texts in written language about being lost. It is a text that highlights the deliberate choice of lostness as well as the lostness that can be thrust upon you:

> "Father, I want right now what's coming to me." So the father divided the property between them. (Luke 15:12 *The Message*)

As the story goes, a man had two sons. There was the more famous younger son and the older, seemingly reclusive one. At times, I find myself relating to both sons, the younger one who ran to Vegas to find himself and the older one who seemed more defined by arrogance and entitlement than sonship, and staying behind and taking everything for granted.

I often wonder why I always considered the younger son the "cool" one. Was it because freedom found him instead of freedom being taken for granted? Or was it just the intrigue of the younger? The younger being the outwardly pitied, yet secretly admired, idol.

The further I travel in life, the harder it gets to distinguish which is the more destructive. Both have addictive natures, both exhibit entitlement, both are selfish, and both erode and break down relationships.

This story could and should also be read as daughters and a mother, a mother and sons, daughters and a father. I'm neither a mother nor a daughter, and I don't know how easy it is to read yourself into a story that doesn't read you. But, mothers and daughters, this is most definitely about you as well.

A man had two sons. One son, the older one, relished his sense of entitlement without understanding the actual inheritance he had right there before him. Entitlement is the enemy of thankfulness and the midwife of arrogance. When the older son's sulk was present, it accompanied the stench of a reluctantly loyal sonship. The family name, to him, was a pathetic badge to wear and a grudging weight to carry. It was evident that the older son wanted a future with his father's stuff but not with the father. As a son of divorce, I understand this. Love is sometimes easier to ascribe to than to enter into. He was lost in his own home, gathering dust in the shadows of dysfunction.

Trust was taken for granted. Familiarity bred and amplified contempt.

The younger son was more obvious, overt in his desire to satisfy himself right now. He takes it. He takes the now and squanders it, literally asking for everything and blowing it on the temporary—albeit fun—yet fleeting. It's always that trash-crash cocktail of the now that entices the most. It was evident that this son wanted the father's stuff but not the father. As a son of divorce, I understand this. Love is sometimes easier to own as a possession than engage with as an emotion. It's easier to own love than to be surrendered to it. He was lost, his home just a memory. His relationship with his father burned for the sake of temporary warmth.

Trust was granted and taken. Contempt bred and amplified unfamiliarity.

And then the younger son leaves. Did he look back? Did he pause wondering if he'd gone too far, wondering if his pride could survive an early return? Did he hesitate? I can remember "running away" as a child, my backpack full of Oreo cookies and Kraft Mac & Cheese, my painted turtle, Jeff, drying out in my hand. I remember hesitating, then pushing forward and getting to the end of the street. Then the panic set in, the fogged-up eyes widened when glancing back, followed by the realization that I was now on my own. My block was only two minutes long, and I had lost my courage to run. The walk of shame back home was accented by, and only made more palatable by, the grace of the Oreo cookies.

But running takes courage. Courage to risk all that was given for something unknown. Is there cowardice in certainty? Empathy sets in for me as I read of the younger son because I can see what he was getting at: a desire to break free, explore, go beyond the boundaries of the father. The fatal flaw, I believe, was that he wanted to leave relationship to do so. What was yet to be known by the younger son was that a trust-filled relationship travels into the unknown together.

Did he look back? Let's wade deeper into this story found in the book of Luke.

> Soon afterward, the younger son gathered everything together and took a trip to a land far away. There, he wasted his wealth through extravagant living.
>
> When he had used up his resources, a severe food shortage arose in that country and he began to be in need. He hired himself out to one of the citizens of that country, who sent him into his fields to feed pigs. He longed to eat his fill from what the pigs ate, but no one gave him anything. (Luke 15:13-16)

This was quite the wake-up call.

I'm sure the younger son had to have been thinking, *What has become of me? What am I doing here? I don't belong here.* The feeling of loneliness and regret deeper than the aching for food. Surely, "one is the loneliest number."[1]

> When he came to his senses, he said, "How many of my father's hired hands have more than enough food, but I'm starving to death! I will get up and go to my father, and say to him, 'Father, I have sinned against heaven and against you. I no longer deserve to be called your son. Take me on as one of your hired hands.'" So he got up and went to his father. (Luke 15:17-20)

He went home, a word he hadn't dared speak for far too long.

Having emptied even the crumbs of his inheritance, he found himself lost in, and restrained by, his mess. He was tangled, unable to reach beyond the quicksand of his excess. An excess that had eroded a trust that had sustained him through his childhood. An excess that limited his access to the Father. What was yet to be known by the younger son is that a pursued and sustained availing of access to the Father will also limit his need for the excess. Excess limits access. But access to love also limits excess.

Some say the younger son had "backslidden." A term we use to make our own self-righteous sin look less staining—sliding is OK, just not backsliding. This term certainly confused me growing up, as some of the best sledding I ever did in the northwestern winters was literally backsliding—sliding backward. As well, this term usually referred to folks who were the kindest to me growing up; those backsliders always seemed to have plenty of time for me. At one point as a child, it almost became inspirational. That is until I was "set straight." That term was "reserved for those who turn their backs on God," I was told. Again, I found this confusing as I'm not sure how we can turn our back on a God who is 360 degrees.

Yet there still existed in the younger son the remnant of trust that was yet to evaporate, and instinctively he knew deep down that the Father would have him back even in the midst of the carnage.

One thing is clear in the story: the younger son had made an ill-advised turn away from his home and his father. This was definitely a temporary setback, and some setbacks last longer than others. But some setbacks are actually more like "release forwards." When two people are ready to restore relationship, it can bring a bond stronger than compliance. Yet choosing to return is as hard as choosing to stay.

We all follow the rabbit holes hoping for a wonderland but end up dreaming of home. How I dream of home. We seem so strong until loneliness enters the soul.

With the scent of pig feces reverberating in his senses, the younger son is possibly speaking aloud for the first time the words, "What am I doing here? I don't belong here." Revelation covered in regret. He stands; he looks to the horizon and goes home to his father.

Damien Rice sings it so well in his song "Trusty and True." Buy this song and take his lyrics to heart.

> And if all that you are
> Is not all you desire,
> Then, come . . .[2]

And then, "When he was still a long way off, his father saw him. His heart pounding, he ran out, embraced him, and kissed him" (Luke 15:20 *The Message*).

NUIT BLANCHE

In the short film *Nuit Blanche*, a man and woman see each other from across the street. It's Paris; the black-and-white film is dense, yet fuller in its lack of color and super-slow-motion depiction. She sets her cigarette down, turns, and stands. He steps to the street, through a puddle. Their eyes are locked—nothing is going to separate them. She walks through the café's glass window as it shatters in the shape of her silhouette. She moves closer. A car strikes, bends, and crumples around the man. He moves closer. Nothing is going to separate them. They reach one another. They embrace. They kiss. Nothing between them.

THEN IT HAPPENS

The father was waiting, for how long no one knows—he sits like a poised raindrop holding on just before it falls free—squinting for just a glimpse of his younger son, a returning silhouette from the shadows. Then it happens: the father rises expectant, the father runs unashamed, the father reaches out before he arrives to his younger son, the father embraces, nothing between them. Heaven couldn't hold him back, nor did it want to. You can't outrun the Father. We cannot outrun the Creator. Why would we want to?

The father committed an audacious act, an initiation of love, annoying the older son, annoying those working the estate, annoying other fathers in the area. Love annoys the proud.

A new precedent was set. But how quickly we forget precedents.

A new precedent was set. From this day fathers should no longer wait. They should always run.

The father's reaction was action, not sitting in his mini-kingdom waiting.

Freedom is not found in the hesitation but in the immediate, instinctual response of love. Trust accelerates when we run to one another.

I wonder: do we as churches drop to our knees, leave our porches, or break a sweat for those who have gone on the run? The arthritis of Christianity is acute and sets in without warning; we ache even in the aborted attempts to reach out. What happens to those who never turn back? Do we leave our temporary homes to go and help them find their eternal lives?

And they embrace.

And nothing separated them.

Was it awkward? Was conversation mumbled, protocol scrambled, eye contact shame-stunted? This brat of a son had taken everything and wasted it. He was reeking of sin. Does sin repel God, or does it attract redemption?

The younger son, wasted, had returned. Is he repentant or just in need—maybe it doesn't matter. He attempts his road-worn, well-rehearsed speech, "Father, I have sinned against heaven and against you. I no longer deserve to be called your son" (Luke 15:21).

But the father, he wasn't listening—just hugging.

The son's repentance was only part of the music of forgiveness.

The father embraces, an uncontrolled, unpredictable, strong embrace. Arms wrapped around the tired, fading carcass of the younger son. The father didn't ask where the son had been sleeping, or if he had been drinking or with whom, what his son was doing. He wasn't listening, just embracing.

Just embracing.

The volume of the father's love was louder than the younger son's guilt.

The volume of God the Father's love is louder than any of our guilt.

I wish I were more like the Father. How often do I demand that someone admit his or her guilt before I even give eye contact? I hold that guilt over them like a guillotine.

NOTHING

When my kids were little, they would occasionally eat too much chocolate, running off and hiding while they gorged themselves. It's a rite of passage to do so, but as a consequence, they would feel ill and want to vomit. Then they'd come out of their sticky hiding place and run toward me covered in vomit, crying. Would I jump back, turn away, and avoid contact? Would I shout, "Clean yourselves up!" and then retreat, wait for them to clean themselves up, and then, possibly, hug them? Did I hesitate? Of course not. I ran to them, dropped to my knees, and embraced them. Nothing separating us. This mess was only temporary.

Sin is only temporary.

God, the Father, doesn't shout from a height. He drops to his knees, covered in the same dirt that you have walked in, a shared road and embraces.

Dan Robins is often quoted as asking us this way: "Do you believe that God loves without condition or reservation, and loves you this moment as you are?"[3]

When we are embraced by the Father we are free. The beautiful oxymoron of a freeing embrace. Then a whisper in the ear of the younger son—it's going to be OK. You are forgiven; now rise up on your feet; let's have a party.

The embrace reestablishes trust.

Then the Father shouts, "My son is here—given up for dead and now alive! Given up for lost and now found!" (Luke 15:24 *The Message*).

To the older son the Father says, "You're with me all the time, and everything that is mine is [still] yours" (Luke 15:31 *The Message*).

And then the older son leaves. In the relationship between the father and the older son, the trust they had was seemingly implicit. But a trust not mutually shared or expressed, nor mutually lived, is deceptive. You possess this trust, but you're not expressing it. Trust is part of your collection, but it's never taken down and utilized, realized. And before you know it, you are either just begrudgingly existing *in* the relationship, or you are flaunting a sense of entitlement because *of* the relationship. Entitlement is soulless. Entitlement is the calcification of trust. Entitlement is the calcification of love.

I focus on the younger son in this chapter as I believe we have, I have, forgotten the incarnational aspect of love, a love that comes and finds. We may talk of love, but do we show it? Do we really mean it? Passive, idle talk of love is restraining and not freeing—the older son reminding us that "everything" of the Father's is still "ours," whatever "ours" means. But "ours" is a collective and nonexclusive—even for those who run.

The porches in our churches and in our lives have gotten crowded with people sitting and talking of inheritance, but love pursues in a relentless search for the other.

Grace is not fetched. Grace goes out and finds.

> *"We got open arms for broken hearts*
> *Like yours my boy, come home again."*[4]

A restorative trust requires presence.

ALL WRAPPED UP

Everything changed that day for the two sons. Life moved from hearing to understanding because they experienced a tangible trust. A good life is not a passive life. This embrace of the Father is beautiful, offensive, and freeing, a raw grace of indiscriminate compassion.

Growing up, I heard often the paraphrased verse that *"nothing* can ever separate us from the love of Christ" (based on Romans 8:39 NLT), yet I find I have plenty of *nothings* in my life that are doing a very good job of separating. Plenty that manages to or is managed to get in the way.

Trust at times is a fleeting bird rustled from the weeds by my flailing faith.

Growing up, these *nothings* were as nuanced and as confusing as my uncle finding the devil in Amy Grant albums to the stash of porn in my friend's garage to the multiple family and church splits. Innumerable *nothings* separating me from love and breaking the trust I had in those I looked up to. Breaking the trust I had in myself.

Both sons had substantial walls of *nothings* separating them from their Father.

The older son hiding in plain sight, doing nothing with what the Father had given him, letting it gather dust. He was lost in his own home. Sometimes we don't have to go very far to feel lost.

The younger son scrambling away and wasting all that had been generously given to him, having ravaged his home's very foundations for the temporary feel of the dirt in his hands now trapped under his broken nails.

Both lacked true relationship with the Father. Trust was an absent conduit in both sons.

Are we like one son or like the other? All wrapped up in ourselves, some out of choice, some out of circumstance. Like a straitjacket cinched up, cutting off the very air we breathe. The leather of its belts restraining growth.

Just like the sons (and daughters) of this story, today we find ourselves:

Wrapped up in fear
Wrapped up in loneliness
Wrapped up in broken relationships
Wrapped up in control
Wrapped up in doubt
Wrapped up in distrust
Wrapped up in feeling worthless
Wrapped up in unknown futures
Wrapped up in unfounded expectations
Wrapped up in entitlement
Wrapped up in failure

Wrapped up in anger
Wrapped up in unforgiveness
Wrapped up in selfishness
Wrapped up in recession
Wrapped up in apathy
Wrapped up in _____
Wrapped up in ourselves

All of our beauty and truth cinched up and smothered, the very heartbeat of our lives hidden away. Odd thing about hidden things: they die away. When hidden things lose their way, the hidden struggles to shine.

But you are loved in this place. Right here—straitjacket and all, having attempted to turn your back on God, who is always facing toward.

You are loved in this place.

WE

We are all embraced so that we can let go of all that we
    are wrapped up in; freed to be.
This is our story. All wrapped up in ourselves, some out of
    choice, some out of circumstance.
This is my story. All wrapped up in myself, sometimes out
    of choice, sometimes out of circumstance.
We are the older and we are the younger sons and
    daughters.
We are the one, and we are the other.

This return to the Father is the raw unwrapping of self, the untangling of a self-induced restraint. The gauze is hardened against the wound; when pulled it may hurt, leaving a mark; scars will form, but healing is at hand.

I

Our straitjackets will cast long shadows. We keep them just in reach; some enshrine them in trophy cabinets for all to see. Others bury them, pretending they never existed.

For some our straitjackets are the ways we left our Father's house, the lives we've lived and continue to live today. For others, it's a story of a prodigal father and the impact of life left behind, but when I'm more raw and honest with myself, I realize my straitjacket is made of both.

I, at times, take my straitjacket back down off the hook and wear it just for the momentary feeling of warmth, but soon the claustrophobia of self gets too much, and I want to be free again. The past and the present sin start stalking and haunting me. Maybe instead of hiding them, I need to keep my straitjackets around and allow them to catch the corner of my eye every once in a while, realizing that the shadows they may cast are no longer shadows of captivity and restraint but a visceral reminder of being freed. Battered icons of freedom instead of something to be feared.

US

This story of the younger and older is the story of us. It is the challenge of the incarnate and what it is to enter into the disconnect, the broken trust. This is a clarion call, a 4-a.m.-alarm-wake-up as a reminder to always begin with an embrace not an accusation.

Jesus came into the mess—our mess—and gave an eternal embrace. Heaven couldn't hold him back, nor did it want to. His arrival and death and resurrection are the ultimate embrace for all. Do we dare to embrace others like this, not controlling access to God through theology and answers—but just rise up and embrace? Do we dare to trust when trust seems only a word?

Tragically, the constraint of exclusion has been proliferated by humanity, and its popularization is our sour contribution to the disconnect between God and humanity.

Know this, we are all included. We are all destined to be free. We belong here; we are no longer foreigners in our own homes, even when we still feel like we are.

We are no longer alone but known.
We are no longer apathetic but courageous.
We are no longer trapped but free.

Again, "nothing separates us from the love of Christ." But, in our lives, there are still plenty, and always will be, very real *nothings* that can and do cause separation, if only temporary. The question is now, with the understanding that we are free, will we allow these *nothings* to become *somethings* that cause a disconnect from God? What will we do with this freedom? How can we, today, rediscover the beauty of a true embrace by the Creator, *nothings* and all? The embrace is the conduit of trust. The lightning rod of restored relationships.

We are the one, the other, and the father.

Three

Trust and Presence

Strangling My Inner Jesus

TV DINNERS WITH A FROG

This was not church; it was far more important. Though, like church, we'd have to sit very still. This was balancing our TV dinners on our laps while watching *The Muppet Show*. My partially frozen gravy, burnt-edged mashed potatoes, and rubbery, scalding hot turkey were never safer; to spill was to miss the Show. This was in the days before microwaves—yes, there was a time.

It has always been a dream of mine to meet the Muppets—whether on the Show or on *Sesame Street*. (If anyone out there has any connections, you know where to find me.) But I want to meet them in action, as I've always been struck, when watching behind-the-scenes footage, by how lifeless such genius characters are when not being puppeteered.

In Brian Jones's beautifully told prologue from his book *Jim Henson: The Biography*,[1] he speaks of a young girl in a red-striped shirt who sings and teases and treats Kermit

30

the Frog not as a discarded piece of Jim Henson's grand-mother's matted, green coat but as a living, breathing, singing friend.

And it hit me: it's not just the puppeteer who brought life to Kermit; it was the young girl, it was a shared love, and it was a mutual trust that brought out the best in them both.

The prologue says that at the end of the song, the young girl and Kermit exchange an honest hug and with eyes alight they say "I love you" to each other. At this point I found myself crying into my coffee and thinking, *This is just a puppet!* But something deeper was rattling about. She could've just seen a puppet. Kermit could've just seen a little girl, but they trusted each other and saw a friend, first.

It was when Kermit knew love and showed love that he became who he was always meant to be.

Trust amplifies love.
Love magnifies trust.

Becoming one who knows love and shows love is the most enduring transformation of any soul. But in order to be-come, we need to know what we are made of and why it is that we were indeed made.

Let's, together, look at two stories. Both describe failures that led to varying degrees of transformation.

BECOMING . . .

"I'm going to tell you who you are, *really* are. You are Peter, a rock. This is the rock on which I will put together my church, a church so expansive with energy that not even the gates of hell will be able to keep it out." (Matthew 16:17-18 *The Message*)

This is the announcement of Peter's becoming. This is *that* moment. Did Peter realize it, or did he only recognize it in hindsight?

Jesus announces his very intention of Peter before Peter had done anything.

Peter was a lovable rogue.
Peter screwed up, often.
Peter was human.
Peter is my hero.

Peter's becoming was beautifully mired with intention and failure, both of which led to his very becoming, a life on the threshing floor.

Peter's humanity was the church's very foundation.

I believe Jesus announces his very intention about you before you have done anything, and I know he learned this from his collaborative Father.

BEFORE, NOT AFTER

Jesus, a relatively unknown man, arrived at the riverside. Rumors of virgins and births and arrogant temple challenges as a boy had preceded him, and a mixture of exclusion and potential had followed him. Rumors were his only followers, so far. His cousin, John, baptized him, and heaven spoke for the filled banks of skeptics to hear: "This is my Son, chosen and marked by my love, delight of my life" (Matthew 3:16 *The Message*).

The crowd that had gathered to gawk now dropped their mouths further. They had all heard it.

Prior to any ministry, to doing any miracles, to speaking words to rattle the soul, to tearing up the veil, God affirms, "My Son." This action is a *before* not an *after*. Loved before any performance. Approval before any proof. True love leads to a true self-becoming.

Understanding the precedence set by God the Father and God the Son, let's get back to Peter's becoming, as it's more tangled and snag-ridden and quite possibly closer to our experience—or at least mine.

PETER 2.0

"Stomp harder." The veracity of the worn and frayed boots colliding on the bowed and scarred wooden floors where the threshing took place; the wheat breaking from its temporary home of the chaff. Hundreds of rattlesnake-like carcasses now strewn. The wheat, now vulnerable, is nourishment.

Peter's life and actions are the threshing and the sifting of his becoming, the separation of the good and bad of our very living, the stomping of living becoming more and more acute. Threshing feels at times like a personal thrashing, a thrashing we all share with Peter.

Peter was a beautiful failure, an overachiever, a friend; authentic, verbal, and young but also the one the future of the church was to be built on.

Peter's becoming was beautifully mired with intention and failure—both consistently leading to his becoming.

I've heard Peter's becoming described as unfortunate, immature, and even silly—"He should've known better!" But I believe that his identity, formed in the trauma of multiple failures, helped form the very essence of who he really was. Not a projection of perfection but a human being through and through. Perfection found in the folds of the flaws.

I now ask you the reader to allow me to look at Peter in the first person: Peter aka Greg. And together we can look at his many highlights masquerading as lowlights.

WATER

> I just left everything behind. Was I sincere or stupid? I'm not sure, but I didn't feel courageous; it's just this man called Jesus seemed to believe in me. It was more of an invitation than a demand when this man called me by name, "Simon" (Peter). At that moment something beyond words compelled me to leave behind my business and to follow this random man whom heaven speaks to. As a lifelong fisherman, this wasn't going to be easy. It's all I've known since being a boy. This was my business, my family, my heritage; these are my boats, my water. My skin shares the texture of the sea. My friends thought I was going insane.[2]

Peter's intention and failure, in the eyes of those gathered, are what begin to lead in that moment to his becoming, they are intrinsically part of his becoming. Becoming often means leaving; leaving a place, a memory, a grudge, and an expectation. Often in these moments that others consider crazy, we begin to find freedom. There is freedom in becoming who you are meant to be.

AIR

> Later having returned, if only briefly, to what I knew best, the sea—how I'd missed that smell, that salty air—and hungry for fish, Jesus suggested for me to "throw the nets to the other side." This carpenter-vagrant telling me, a fisherman, where to throw nets? Doesn't he know who I am? (In hindsight, he could've asked me the same thing.) On the verge of telling him I knew best, I decided to go with humility—something that didn't come easy—and I threw the nets on the wrong side. The fish climbed and thrashed, and there were so many they tore my nets.[3]

Peter's frustration yet intention to follow is evident, even when he knew best, both frustration and intention leading to his becoming.

DIRT

> We were hanging around together, eating and listening to our Rabbi, Jesus, telling stories that we'd never heard before in ways that we'd never heard before. Then in an instant our Rabbi is on the ground in front of us, reaching for our road-weary, dirt-covered feet. He wants to wash my feet? I cut him off mid-sentence saying, "You will never wash my feet!"

He looked up at me with a determined patience—I was no stranger to this look—and said, "Unless I wash you, you won't have a place with me."

I immediately stood, wanting to strip off, saying, "Lord, not only my feet but also my hands and my head!" That didn't go down well; I'd missed the point again. He had been speaking of humility not coverage.[4]

Wash every inch of me. Peter had such persistence and desire to be in the middle of it all. Even in his failure to see everything clearly, his intention was part of his becoming.

WIND

I was tired and my eyes were definitely seeing things. As the waves rose and fell, I kept getting glimpses of a man *on* the water. Impossible. But then the impossible called my name. I looked over my shoulder, wondering if Jesus knew any other Peters. He called out for me to step onto the water, the very water that, in shallower shores, had killed many of my friends. I'm not sure if it was because everyone was watching or because Jesus was calling, but I stepped out; the surface splashed like a puddle. As I walked closer to him, I got more confident yet more afraid—two emotions that were never far from me. I was stepping farther and farther from safety, from my security, or was it toward? And then it happened (even in the middle of a miracle I was struggling to trust Jesus). I began to sink. I know how quickly this can happen, how quickly a man can drown, and I could only just reach with my eyes and stretch with my arms toward him. His hand met me where I was, and together we continued our journey of the impossible.[5]

We can only learn of the strong reach of love when we have ventured beyond safety. Peter's intention compelled him upon the surface of the sea. His wrestle of faith in that moment, some would call failure; yet both faith and failure are part of his becoming.

BLOOD

I didn't hesitate. I scrambled and grabbed the sword out of its sheath, and I attacked the soldier. They wanted to take my friend away for crimes that he hadn't committed; they wanted to kill him—this couldn't end well. The sword was lighter than expected as I cut through the soldier's ear. I heard my name, again, but the tone had changed, I'd gone too far. But . . . but . . . my excuses fell silent as Jesus lifted the soldier's ear and replaced it.[6]

For Peter, intention and failure were both part of his becoming.

(A quick aside, I would love to hear the soldier's recounting this story over the family dinner that night. A routine arrest, a madman cutting his ear off, the criminal putting his ear back. "Pass the potatoes, please." Was this the beginning of the soldier's own becoming?)

TEARS

It wasn't a week to be proud of; in so many
moments I failed my friend. I slept while he
bled alone that night in the garden, only me-
ters away; I disowned him—my friend—when
I was afraid and more than once; I hid while
he lay dead in his grave. My heart still breaks
afresh, and my tears fail to fall from worn out
tear ducts—some of guilt, some of joy—as I look
back and realize who I was with and what was to
become of my friend, my God.[7]

Peter's intentions and failures followed and led him everywhere; all were part of his becoming. Peter's actions were
swift and impulsive; he was rash yet humble; he was reluctant yet still called. We all are. But Peter's failures or lack of
faith were nothing compared to Jesus' love.

It is in love where Peter truly becomes.
It is in love where we truly become.

SPIRALING PROCESS

*Who do you become when the world doesn't unfold in the
way you think it should? You are designed as a contribution; a contribution that seeks to present itself. What is it in
you that is a core contribution that breaks through?*
—Jim McNeish

Our lives are a continual process of becoming. Our living is
our becoming; it is our emergence as who we were always
meant to be. But who we are is not just on the horizon—it
is the heat of the sun in the day and the cold of the night

on our feet; it is with us now. Trust in the Creator is a belief that we are, in this very moment, as we are meant to be. Yes, we are all becoming and evolving and transforming, and beauty is exploding from us in the midst of storms, and it can be ugly, and it can be breathtaking, but it's in all of this becoming that we are most like ourselves. We need to be most like ourselves.

There is a peace that emerges in trusting the becoming and the God of the becoming, a trust that brings a peace knowing I am as I am meant to be.

Yet when I was younger—and yes, still at times (far too many times in my seesaw living)—that peace, that trust, takes the nearest emergency exit. And I find myself spiraling toward the terra firma.

STRANGLING MY INNER JESUS

I was similar to Peter my whole life: an eager, well-intentioned failure who would rather risk and get it wrong than not risk at all; a life defined in the wrestle between trust and its seemingly ever-present twin, distrust.

My personal becoming was announced with a hand around my throat. At the age of eighteen, I found myself standing in a renowned haven for drug addicts in Geneva, Switzerland. To say I was just standing there would be misleading. Our presence was intentional.

We were in a park full of comatose homeless people, drug addicts, and prostitutes. I felt out of my depth—my safe Michigan upbringing a seemingly useless life vest in the quicksand of my inexperience.

As I looked around I saw the pain and confusion and lostness, and I felt helpless. I both yearned and feared to reach
the heart of the physical needs right in front of me—to
have an honest response. So we did the obvious . . . we did
a drama. And I was Jesus—a blue-eyed, blond-haired, mul-
leted Jesus. Such an innocent arrogance. Or is it an arrogant innocence? The drama not the mullet, possibly both.

Halfway through the drama, they placed me/Jesus on
the cross, and I fashioned my body into the perfect cross
shape—one that I am proud to announce that I had prac-
ticed many times in my childhood, (my motives not being
the purest, as I had seen many a "Jesus" get all the attention of the girls around Easter).

This was my moment, my debut, my . . . Do you know the
feeling you get when your eyes are closed but you feel
something is coming at you? That sense you get when
your body is about to be impacted? Well that something
and that sense was a man called Anton, and he was running right at me.

A few things happened in quick succession. First and
foremost, I consulted my WWJD bracelet and truly wondered if I should get off my cross and leg it. I wonder if, in
the words of a friend, it would've served me better asking,
"What Would Judas Do" in this situation?

Anton was six feet eight inches tall, with torn clothes, hair
streaked blond and pink, and looking as if he'd slept a lifetime
on the streets. Anton was a mountain of man and the mountain was on the move, running full throttle at me shouting
in broken English—"Who the f**k are you?!" over and over
again. I was a terrified "Jesus," but I held character, kind of.

My friends, fellow missionaries, and community of drama-
tists, seeing that I was under threat, parted like the Red
Sea. Anton grabbed me by the scruff of my neck, took
me off the cross, and slammed me into the stone wall
behind me. Now, I was a totally terror-filled "Jesus," I was
consumed by fear, but I also knew that where I ran would
define who I would become. I stood strong-ish, I didn't
move—nor could I, I was paralyzed as his spittle hit my
face and he shouted, "Who the f**k are you?" I answered
feebly, "Greg and, um, Jesus."

I don't know what could've been going through his
drug-induced mind at this point, but the answer surprised
him, and he said, "What the f**k did Jesus ever do for
me?" I had no answer. I just stood there doing my best not
to continue freaking out. I just looked at him, and he just
looked back.

Over the next three weeks, we continued doing dramas
and either freaking out the drug addicts or aiding in their
trips, but I also spent hours every day with Anton. Anton
was homeless. Anton was a heroin addict. Anton was a
male prostitute. Anton was living with AIDS. Anton was
dying from AIDS. Anton would change my life.

I was a lower-middle-class kid from an all-white, safe
neighborhood in Michigan. I'd never talked to a male
prostitute although, as a young boy, I remember seeing
an older female prostitute through the car's rear window:
Chicago, 1979, Rush Street, she was African American, tall,
stark, and beautiful, looking tired as she leaned against the
pharmacy wall. I didn't know anything about the homeless,
heroin, or AIDS. But Anton was human, and so am I.

But I felt as if I'd failed my team, God, and Anton because Anton never prayed the "sinner's prayer," never understood the four spiritual laws, and only had one sober day while I was in Geneva, and it happened on my day off! Addicts do not get days off, and I really wished I hadn't missed his clean day. Was God any less with him whether high or clean? I don't think so.

Over the following weeks of walking and sitting and laughing, we connected and began to trust each other. Anton and I grew to know each other. We shared a very common life path; he, too, felt forgotten, alone and abandoned, angry and incomplete. He, too, wondered, as my biological father and I have, if he was meant for this world. On the last day as we did our final clown routine (when will I ever learn?) and loaded onto the bus, Anton was nowhere to be seen. I was gutted. I wanted to say a last good-bye.

As the bus began to pull away, people began to shout, "It's Anton, pull over!" Sure enough, there he was chasing the bus down the middle of the street, no fear. We pulled over, and I got out to thank him for all he had taught me about God and for what he had taught me about myself. He stopped my words short as he began to take off his outer layer of clothing, a torn black and purple jumper, saying, "I want you to have this." I, of course, said no as this was one of the many layers he needed to sleep rough. It was all he owned, and it was cold at night. He replied, "This is the only thing I have that my mother gave me before I left home, and I know it will be safe with you." And as he hugged me, he added, "Thank you for being Jesus to me." I could've said—and now wish I had said—the same thing to him. I still have that jumper.

Anton had been able to relate and trust this limited version of a pretend Jesus before him more honestly than I could've ever imagined performing or living.

This mission trip was mutual. Actually, maybe, we should stop calling it mission and call it living. Calling it mission has immunized us from connecting, from being, from living.

Intention and failure were both part of my becoming. Anton's love was the threshing, my personal thrashing, whether it be a strong hand on the throat or the wrestle and collision of a life lived with intention.

I learned those weeks of the visceral connection of becoming incarnate. When trust is established, love is known.

It is when I knew love and showed love that I became who I was always meant to be.

It was in love where I truly became.
It is in love where we truly become.

I don't know and may never know what happened to Anton after that summer in Geneva. I often wish I could revisit that time, leave the drama in the bag and just walk over with a coffee, courage, and some clean clothes. I still cry when I think of that lovely mountain of man and am eternally thankful for what he taught me.

FRIEND OF FRAUDS

Peter's becoming . . .
My becoming . . .
Your becoming . . .

We all have that something-fast-approaching fear of becoming. We all feel like frauds at times. What Peter may have been saying deep down when denying his friend and Rabbi is, "I'm afraid to live without you, Jesus." His bravado and denial helped keep the reality of Jesus' going away at a distance. And then Peter ran away.

Maybe I was saying to Anton, "I'm afraid to speak to you. My acting and performing will keep the reality of your needs, my needs, at a controllable distance." And then I ran away. Twenty years later, I realize that I was trying to keep both Anton and my own mess at a controllable distance. Because of Anton, when I look now, I see my pain and confusion and lostness in me first.

Do I allow my life's rituals to bring freedom, or do they create a controllable distance? Does my faith bring freedom, or does it create a controllable distance?

I see now that playing Jesus was safer than being Jesus. And I see now that Jesus would've had a lot more in common with Anton than me; his honesty, his humanity, his love that was unafraid to confront me, to change me, to show me that being Jesus is far more important than playing him.

Are we committed to the forgiving threshing of love? A threshing that breaks the skin and reveals our true selves?

It is when you know love and show love that you become who you were always meant to be. And in this you're not alone.

Jesus became so that we could become.

He had equal status with God but didn't think so much of himself that he had to cling to the advantages of that status no matter what. Not at all. When the time came, he set aside the privileges of deity and took on the status of a slave, became *human*! Having become human, he stayed human. It was an incredibly humbling process. He didn't claim special privileges. Instead, he lived a selfless, obedient life and then died a selfless, obedient death—and the worst kind of death at that—a crucifixion. (Philippians 2:5-8 *The Message*)

Jesus became so we could become.

It is in his love where we truly become. And many times this love comes from unlikely places and in unlikely ways. Jesus still walks among our daily denials, a friend to the frauds, committed to our continued becoming, our being. Your failures or lack of faith are nothing compared to his love.

Peter, after years of living as the cracked rock on which a trustworthy church is built, after experiencing denials and miracles, after learning to live without his closest friend, writes, "Love one another as if your lives depended on it" (1 Peter 1:22-25 *The Message*).

Becoming one who knows love and shows love is the most enduring transformation of any soul.

Four

Trust and Fear

The Day Everything Changed

SNOW

My first journey to Belfast, Northern Ireland, was in the late 1980s. This was the decade of *Knight Rider*, the Commodore 64, Milli Vanilli, and "I'm a Pepper" T-shirts. This was the decade that those who hadn't grown up in wish they had and those who did are only admitting to now.

I arrived in Belfast just in time for a cup of tea. There always seems to be time for tea on this island, and not just the one. We sat in the window bay of the "good room," myself with a sugar-filled tea—the coffee revolution a lifetime away—and the elderly couple who were hosting me, the trio of us spreading strawberry jam on our heavy scones. And then it caught the corner of my eye, quickly filling the whole of my now very wide eyes; we had been invaded. More specifically the elderly couple's front garden looked like a war zone, soldiers spilling over the small stone walls on bended knee—a front line in a front yard. The old woman looked at me with a gentle, worn smile and passed me another scone saying, "Welcome to Belfast."

To know Belfast is to love Belfast. And I love Belfast. It is a beautiful and broken city, with hope and heartache around every corner.

My good friend, Seán (pronounced Shawn), grew up in West Belfast in the 1970s and 1980s.[1] He is from a Catholic family. He has brothers who attempted to join the paramilitary organization called the Irish Republican Army (IRA), and cousins who did. Peace was elusive in his neighborhood. And trust beyond the family only a slowly evolving construct.

On his streets and in his schools, he inherited the idea that those in East Belfast, predominately Protestant at the time, were different and that the British soldiers were his enemies, that "they" are not like "us." Their scars deeper yet the same, just below the surface—prejudice and misunderstanding and inheritance and arrogance and mutual injustice.

But that all changed thirty years ago when it began to snow.

Every day at recess in Seán's school, the hundred or so young men would collect stones and throw them, along with insults, at the soldiers as they passed by on their daily patrols. But today was different.

As they looked out at the snow falling, they started scheming. Today at recess they would do something different. A plan was hatched. The bell rang and they raced outside, gathering up as much snow as they could, compacting it and rolling it into balls. Piles of snowballs rising up around the fenced-off playground.

Meanwhile, the soldiers began to approach, as they did every day, from around the corner, and they could sense something was different. It was quiet on the usually loud playground. As they turned the corner they realized why. The students launched their snowballs, hundreds of them rising and arching over the chain-link fences and falling onto the ten soldiers' heads. Snowballs instead of stones. Snowballs instead of insults. Snow has a way of silencing the noise.

The soldiers dove behind a small stone wall and took their rifles off their shoulders. The students froze. My friend thinking, *This is the end. This is how it ends for me, in a snowball fight in a playground.* The students could just see the tops of the heads of the soldiers and the tips of their rifles; they could see the guns emerging, getting ready.

But when the soldiers stood up, they were no longer holding guns. They were holding snowballs of their own.

The playing field was now fully leveled. Rocks are nothing to bullets, but a snowball is as a snowball does. Rather than swords turning to ploughshares, it was shotguns turning to snowballs.

And there and then, for twenty minutes, a hundred students and ten soldiers had a ginormous snowball fight. No longer strangers, no longer enemies, no longer an "us" or a "them." Peace found in a fight. And there in that place, a questioning and wrestling of an inherited distrust began to emerge in Seán's heart.

Everything changed that day as Seán realized, *They are just like us!*

Trust, like the first flower of spring breaking through the ice, emerging when they least expected it. Trust is not forced; trust surprises us.

The snow was what they had in common, and together they found the change. When we seek the common, we will find the change.

The essence of trust began to emerge that day on the streets of Belfast.

On that day Seán's curiosity was heightened to a peace that he was being newly acquainted with. Peace took him by surprise, and from that day on, he began to pursue peace and establish trust in the midst of a troubled city, in the midst of a young, troubled heart, in the midst of fear.

My friend Seán has spent his adult life working in the area of reconciliation and establishing trust in the beautiful yet fragmented city of Belfast; I'm so glad it snowed on Belfast in the winter of his youth.

JACKHAMMER

Fear exists in society today; there is no denying that. We exist in a culture of fear—whether it's self created or projected, violence or the threat of it, wars or their rumors. Being overwhelmed by these fears is quite easy. Fear simmers on a low boil and eventually overflows.

Fear takes on many forms from bullying to binge drinking, relationships to exams, fear of failure to loneliness, broken families to broken hearts, receding hairlines to recession, from an excess of expectations to an excess of success.

49

My parents used to say that it's easier to grow up today; they were wrong. (As a parent now, I realize this is actually possible—being wrong that is.) Everything is far more accessible. It's far easier to get a quick fix from fear. It's far easier today to numb ourselves from living.

When fear prevails, we can be consumed, covered, smothered, barely surviving under the weight. Our skin, our being, our very soul aching for more.

What are your fears?

Nothing disintegrates trust like fear. Fear is a jackhammer to the foundations that we have built our families, our communities, our churches, and our lives on. When we fear, we struggle to trust. We must somehow overcome the fear of trusting. Yet, must we know fear in order to know trust?

I know that it would be a popular thing to say that a life without fear is a full life lived in peace, but I believe that fear may also be a gift. What if we just embraced it? Would it cease to be fear? Fear focuses the moment, drives us deeper into our created courage, and enables us to avoid avoiding the issue. The questions, the ugliness, the reality of my loneliness, my anger, my, my, my . . . it's all there but so easily dodged until fear comes and amplifies it, like the pain of a splinter under a fingernail or a harsh cough in the silence.

What do my fears say about me? What does the way I deal with my fears say about me? Can I ever truly trust if my fears resonate more loudly than the love I have in my life? Or can my fears actually deepen my trust by teaching me how to risk more in loving?

JESUS FAILED

"Jesus Failed." I stood there dumbfounded as the fifteen-year-old boy looked up at me with tears in his eyes. He was afraid. So was I. Seeing the look on my face, he repeated it again, this time with a bit more caution in his tone: "Jesus failed." In an instant, years of apologetics came flooding back to me; stories upon stories that could "prove" him wrong reared their heads; a cold, electric surge of defensiveness shot up my spine . . . but I had no words. I looked back at him and just said, "Why?"

It didn't take long for this young man to unfold his story of broken trusts: the divorced family, the bullying in school, and the overwhelming feeling that he was un-wanted and anonymous. A walking statistic. It took even less time for him to articulate that entering his church only made him feel more like a foreigner. This faith that had belonged to his parents and his grandparents seemed out of rhythm with his inner metronome. A spiri-tual compass that could no longer detect, let alone trust, due north.

I took a deep breath, and in a moment abducted by grace, I managed not to get in the way of God and said simply:

"Jesus has not failed you; I have."

I was not there for you when you needed me most. We were not there for you when you needed us most.

Fear permeates our lives and societies today, and it under-mines trust. Fear causes us to react in ways of the gut—fight and flight and freeze—but also to reach and love. We need to rediscover trust in the midst of fear.

A SKEPTICAL EYE

Allow me to state the obvious. Over the years, our trust in institutions and relationships has been eroded. Trust has been relegated to the sidelines of our lives. It seems that we have become good at negotiating levels of relationship without actually trusting any longer. We look with a skeptical eye and believe with a list of contingencies. Could we even name on one hand the people whom we would fall from a height into the arms of? Could we name on one hand the number of institutions that we would fall from a height into the arms of? Personally, I struggle to. Maybe it's just me, but I have a hunch I may not be alone.

Trust in individuals is directly related to trust in God. We may not want this to be so, but it's true. When we fail—and we all do—others can feel like God is failing them, and we can feel like God is failing us. When churches fail, trust in the God of those churches erodes. We are all flawed; therefore, churches are flawed. It's natural, it's human nature; but that's why redemption was needed, and that's why Jesus came to rebuild a trust that faith had failed to fulfill. And collectively, if we're being really honest with ourselves, we have done a great job of setting ourselves back to those pre-incarnational days. Those who find themselves outside of the church or outside of the relationships of Christians say, "If it weren't for Christians and the church I might be able to believe in God." I get it. I have felt the same way. I've emerged from a shattered history of broken relationships in both family and church.

My sense of frustration at times has morphed into a sense of loss that settles begrudgingly into apathy.

And now this broken trust creates casualties, heightening the overwhelming feeling of being forgotten.

SYMBIOTIC

When God's conduits lack love, the logical conclusion many come to is that the God they worship lacks it too. It almost seems like it's easier to have faith these days than to actually trust. Whether that be in relationships: "I have faith in them, but I don't know if I can really trust them." Or in God, where we can spend plenty of time believing and not much time trusting.

When did it become OK for faith and trust to be separated? We may say that you can't have one without the other, but we as Christians have sadly proved that trust and faith can exist without each other. Yet separated, neither will thrive; and, eventually, severed from one another they will wither.

Both, when together, are inexorably linked to the incarnate. Jesus came to redeem us all—mission accomplished—but Jesus also came to reestablish a trust eroded by centuries of God-followers who had gotten really good at faith but who were incredibly distrustful. I myself am most certainly included.

I believe it's time for a fresh incarnation that focuses on trust. I believe trust is the road less traveled to authentic faith. We can no longer propagate the snake oil medicine of faith without actually being trustworthy. Faith can no longer be a cop-out for not building a trustworthy relationship, worthy of a King. Redemption was the reconnection; we can no longer live as estranged lovers.

This book is a journey of trust for both of us. It looks at how we can become active restorers of trust between God and us, and between us and us.

But this is not for the fainthearted, as I believe trust is harder to establish than faith. The author of the Book of Hebrews wrote, "Faith is confidence in what we hope for and assurance of what we do not see" (Hebrews 11:1 NIV), yet trust is based on what we do see—and seeing, when it comes to trust, is believing. Believing needs to be backed by action, and that is where we come in. When it comes to our lives, believing in God is just not enough. Real, raw, tangible trust is at a crisis-level deficit in this wonder-filled world, a world where faith has sadly become anecdotal.

As we establish trust in God, we will see faith grow. When we prioritize trust, faith will last beyond the crisis. Pursue trust, and relationship will follow; depth of faith will follow. They are symbiotic.

The disciples were called to follow in faith a man they may have heard of but had only just met, and yet, faith was enough to release their nets from their grips. But it's when they began to trust this man made of flesh that they really began to understand what this whole faith and kingdom of God looks like.

Faith causes us to follow; trust causes us to participate.

Some may and should argue that a faith based on the tangible trust of others is a weaker faith as faith shouldn't be dependent on what we can see. I would argue, however, that faith without trust is one that can easily exist in the ether, one that can easily keep us in our cozy caves with our own exclusive rituals and languages. All of which I have tragically become fluent in.

Can there be faith without trust? Can trust in God exist in a faithless void? No. Faith finds its traction in trust. Trust is the skin on the bones of faith. Trust is the hard currency of faith; it solidifies faith. Tangible trust grounds our faith in reality. Do I need to see a miracle to trust that miracles can actually happen? Yes, I do—I'm that kinda guy. And Jesus got that. Jesus gets this. His ministry is a master class showing that this is possible for you. Effectively saying, "Here I am, in the flesh, trust me." How much harder would it be today for us to believe, to trust, if redemption had been done from afar? Jesus' incarnation was not just about redemption, it was about reestablishing trust between God and humanity. Jesus' ministry was not devoid of the incarnate, nor can ours be.

I want to get back to being a people and church that are trustworthy. If you want to see your city renewed and your relationships flourish, then spend time building trust. If you want to see others coming into a lasting relationship with an unseen God, then be the trusted and incarnate walking alongside and showing the way.

A restored trust restores.

> By opening up to others, you'll prompt people to open up with God. . . . In a word, what I'm saying is, *Grow up.* You're kingdom subjects. Now live like it. Live out your God-created identity. Live generously and graciously toward others, the way God lives toward you. (Matthew 5:16, 48 *The Message*)

Five

Trust and Posture

Living with Change

OXYGEN

I had never tasted something so delicious in my life. It was like sunshine had a flavor.

I could never breathe very well. And breath being one of those necessities, this was a big concern for my mother. This was "back in the day" before inhalers in your pocket and the ability to open up the lungs at a moment's notice for just a bit more air. I'd often find myself at the base of a tree, eyes glazed, seeing colors that I didn't know existed as the air slowly seeped out of my weakened lungs. And then with patience and awkward positions, sweet relief would arrive, and I'd be climbing again.

And then we went camping.

The campsite was on the shore of Mackinac Island. The bitter ash of a leftover fire was palatable, the absence of sugar acute for us boys. We had a list: no milk, no sugar, no fresh-cut grass. All of these would cause reactions in us that would end the Norman Rockwell setting around the fire. But then my uncle, a hippie formerly of the unknown band Uncle Zip, said, "I heard that if you pray to Jesus he can heal you." We looked around, poked the fire a few times, and shrugged our shoulders, my Mom interjecting, "OK, let's pray." Isaiah 53:5 was spoken out—the first time I'd heard this verse (soon to be heard more, thanks to the black-and-yellow clad 1980s Christian hair band "Stryper"; more from them later)—and in the King James Version no less:

> But he was wounded for our transgressions, he was bruised for our iniquities: the chastisement for our peace was upon him, and with his stripes we are healed. (Isaiah 53:5 KJV)

And then we prayed.

The next morning, greeting our usual bowl of cornflakes with water on top, was a miracle: glasses of milk and a box of doughnuts. You can call it faith, or you can call it ignorance, or you can call it both . . . maybe they are intrinsically linked. But one thing was true: my mother trusted that if God said it, then God meant it, and our whole household was dragged along for the ride, albeit a more hyper and sugar-induced one. Freedom had a new name that day—doughnuts. And also another—trust.

I stood taller that day and still stand tall at times these days. My physical, emotional, and spiritual posture had shifted; something in me had changed. I saw things differently.

I still have an inhaler. I still get out of breath. I have a son who does the same. Do I believe any less in the miracle? Yes, at times. Do I believe that miracles can be problematic? Yes, at times. They demand faith, and they demand trust, and at times they provide results; but at times miracles lie dormant, and that can rattle me and my faith. Does this cause me to believe any less in the God of miracles? Sure, at times of course it does, as a miracle is linked to the source. But, regardless of the miracle, my posture that day experienced a metamorphosis when I trusted beyond myself, when I trusted my family and God.

Do I believe that miracles, when they find us, can reshape our perspective on living and life? Absolutely. It all depends on how you describe a miracle. It could be the reflection on a glacial lake; the deaf hearing for the first time; forgiveness; a poem read in a low, graveled voice; or a doughnut. It all depends on how you describe a miracle and what questions a miracle answers, or what questions go unanswered in a miracle.

SIT UP STRAIGHT

My whole childhood was spent in the presence of clicking fingers, snapping at my posture. Sit up straight. You'll never walk right if you sit like that. If the wind blows, you'll be stuck in that hunched position. Then I met my wife, a ballet dancer in her youth—she slouched! Redemption comes in so many ways.

Posture is developed over the years and worn down over years. The way we live and move affects the way we move and live; apparently, it's science. Although I wouldn't know, as my science only extends to a few cracked Petri dishes and one very hot Bunsen burner. There was a lot of smoke that day in room 210, but it wasn't my fault, I promise.

What's your posture like right now as you read (or listen to) this book?

What posture do you assume? What posture do you feel you assume?

A few more questions, and you won't be graded. What are the external forces that affect your posture, both positive and negative?

What are the *internal* forces that affect your posture, both positive and negative?
When I'm insecure, I avoid eye contact; my body follows.
When I'm confident, I seek eye contact; my body follows.
When I'm angry, I avoid physical connection.
When I'm happy, I reach out and pursue connection.
When I'm sad, my hand travels over my face.
When I'm tired, I slouch.
When I've had enough of the day, I lean back, sigh, and close my eyes. Everyone around me understands.

Again, the way I live and move affects the way I move and live.

So, does it really matter what my posture is externally?

Let's take it a step further: if you were to X-ray your spirit, what posture do you feel it would have?

Does it really matter what my posture is internally?

BEFORE AND AFTER

> Jesus was teaching in one of the synagogues on the Sabbath. A woman was there who had been disabled by a spirit for eighteen years. She was bent over and couldn't stand up straight. When he saw her, Jesus called her to him and said, "Woman, you are set free

from your sickness." He placed his hands on her and she straightened up at once and praised God." (Luke 13:10-13)

The Message says it like this, "'Woman, you're free!' He laid hands on her and suddenly she was standing straight and tall, giving glory to God" (Luke 13:13 *The Message*).

If it were only this easy, right? But what we don't see is the before and after of this miraculous story. The Bible is great on getting right to the heart of things, but setting up context and continuity is not one of its strongest suits—something I suffer from as well. One guy once described listening to me as like watching a Quentin Tarantino movie—compelling yet confusing, but it all seems to make sense in the end. (I guess I just need to amp up the gratuitous violence now, and you need to skip to the ending.)

What was the before and after of this story of restored posture? How did her posture change physically, emotionally, and spiritually that day?

For eighteen years she had been afflicted with this level of debilitating arthritis, yet she still had to live. Twisted she had to beg for food. Bent she refused to break, in that forward, fused, bent position. Did she pursue the Messiah on that day using the cracks in the cobbled streets as her map, the grooves in the dirt caused by rain as her guide? These eroded markings nothing but a nuisance to those who walked upright, but to her they were a detailed GPS. Or was she swept up unknowingly in a crowd wanting to get near the teacher to hear his voice firsthand? What was her stoop like, the place she attempted to get comfortable, daily waiting for the generosity of strangers? Was she moved often due to her deformed state? When was the last time she had eye contact with anyone?

And then a voice echoes throughout the courtyard; it was the mysterious man's, and though he could be speaking to anyone, she knew he was speaking right to her.

She had been seen. It had been years since she had been seen.

And then a hand, rough from years of carpentry, rests on her bended shoulder.

She had been touched. It had been years since she had been touched.

She had been healed. It had been years since she had stood straight.

Had she even asked for healing? Healing has a way of surprising us—by showing up and by not showing up. Do I have a faith equally in the lack of healing as much as in those fleeting healing moments? It depends on how you define healing.

This woman now stood and stretched, her back arching, seeing the treetops again. Her arms stretched in one of those amazing stretches where your whole body goes warm and you just exhale.

She flexed and did not snap. Her muscles listened for the first time in eighteen years. Her neck swiveled as birds flew past and as onlookers gawked at her.

Her eyes locked on this young man of miracles. Eye contact, how she had missed that. And to be met with such joy-filled and caring eyes; she knew then that this moment would never leave her.

The stunning song "Gabriel and the Vagabond," by Foy Vance, though not explicitly about this woman of posture, I believe captures its essence as only great art can.[1] Buy this song and enjoy a beautiful story of a man who reaches out and gently whispers hope to a woman finding it hard to cope.

Everything had changed for her. A trust severed by decades of being relegated to the gutters of society was emerging as her skeleton realigned, as her heart realigned.

She now saw the world differently, from different angles. And her world would never see her as the same again, either.

She had a hope return that had been evaporated from her life, her future now radically realigned.

Her physical posture healed, her internal posture began to restore.

Postures change as they encounter the living God.
Posture affects perception.
Posture affects realities.

THE WRESTLE

But the problem isn't just the belief and the miracle; it's the life and wrestle in the posture of living it afterward. It's trusting beyond the miracle or despite it.

What happens when the elation subsides, how do we live with posture change?

I can walk—now what?
I can see—now what?
I breathe—now what?
I've been forgiven—now what?
I have forgiven—now what?

The problem is that good posture is easily forgotten.

Bad posture is easily fallen back into.

I wonder, did the old woman habitually hunch over though healed? Was it a muscle memory? Did she look down in order to recognize where she was? Did she look down in order to recognize those she knew, the landscape of their feet known better than the features of their faces? Did the healing make life harder for her? Was her livelihood now eradicated? Did she need to enroll in some upskilling courses? Did she bang her head on doorways and arch- ways that up until then had expanded above her? Did she permit this life-altering experience to become just a tale, folklore? Did it become just another story that she would tell at dinner among the moans of her family, rolling theirs eyes in a chorus of "not this story again"? Would its significance have been diluted by the failing postures of a healing forgotten?

Should we always seek healing, or are truer peace and trust found living outside of the miracle?

SLOUCH

I've had the incredible opportunity to travel to and work alongside many of the poorest in Africa and Eastern Europe, and the old adage is more than true: I receive far more than I could ever give. While in these countries for far-too-short journeys, I can feel my spiritual, emotional, and physical posture realign, or align for the first time. At these times, I see what is really important in life, how accumulation is just a barbed dream state of the weak, how stuff is not joy. I sleep better, I listen better, I serve more, and I smile more. But give me three weeks (if that) back home and my posture slouches, I accumulate, I ignore, I am restless, and I am grumpy.

Why is it when we are most free that we crave our personal prisons?

Do we always revert to slouching in the spirit, or is there a way we can we retain an uprightness, ready for action? My concern is that we experience life and God and our postures get restored to an Eden state, then we forget and slouch again.

In this place, together, our individual and collective postures' theme song becomes less like the hymn "Amazing Grace" and more like the 1950s atomic bomb public service announcement *Duck and Cover*.

DUCK AND COVER

In 1951 the United States Civil Defense released an official film called *Duck and Cover* to be shown in schools, training the children of the day the best ways to respond and survive an atomic explosion.

This nine-minute animated and live-action film featured an unassuming and shy turtle named Bert; a confident male narrator; and scenes of children diving into street gutters, under desks, and under tractors, covering their heads with their hands, as well as families diving under newspapers and picnic blankets.

From the narrator's transcript:

> We must know how to duck and cover in a school bus, or in any other bus or streetcar. Duck and cover! Don't wait, duck away from the windows fast, the glass may break and fly through the air and cut you.
>
> Sundays, holidays, vacation time, we must be ready every day all the time to do the right thing if the atomic bomb explodes. Duck and cover! This family knows what to do just as your own family should. They know that even a thin cloth helps protect them. Even a newspaper can save you from a bad burn. But the most important thing of all is to duck and cover yourself, especially where your clothes do not cover you.
>
> No matter where we live in the city or country, we must be ready all the time for the atomic bomb. Duck and cover! That's the first thing to do, duck and cover. The next important thing to do after that is to stay covered until the danger is over.[2]

Is the body of Christ hiding under picnic baskets? Are burrs from the undergrowth collecting on the bride's dress?

Are we cowering in the spirit? Should we actually be singing "Duck and Cover" in our worship instead? Are we already? Have we allowed fear to replace amazing grace? Control to replace love? Systems or structures to replace trust and faith?

Corinthians two ways, both of which are compelling:

> If I speak in the tongues of men or of angels, but
> do not have love, I am only a resounding gong or a
> clanging cymbal. (1 Corinthians 1:13 NIV)

> If I speak with human eloquence and angelic ecstasy
> but don't love, I'm nothing but the creaking of a rusty
> gate. (1 Corinthians 13:1 *The Message*)

Are we in danger of becoming gong-bangers: making up
our own language and rules, bastardizing God's design
just to accumulate power? Have we become collectors of,
become curators of creaking, rusty gates?

God created language, and the tongues of humanity have
communicated with one another to create and to innovate,
but have we as the church become anti-linguists, unable
to communicate any longer with the "others" and "theys"
and "thems" who are not "us's"?

When did distrust become the default setting of the body
of Christ; has the body become a weary, twisted bit of
folklore? Has our posture become so insular that we are no
longer able to love?

When did love become so complex?

Ugh. Too many questions, I agree. But I ask because I
need to know. I guess I just get fatigued by all of my
superiority junk. As if junk has rankings. It's my "I-know-
better-than-you mentality again, playing a holier-than-thou
part instead of just living [my] own part" (Luke 6:41-42 *The
Message*).

THE UGLY TRUTH

The subversive miracle within the miracles of Jesus was not just that a person was standing taller or a boy was breathing easier but that their healings were challenging church and society and how they saw—or refused to see—those around them before the healing and/or despite it. The miracles of Jesus challenge an ill-informed church that says, "you're sick because of the sin." Those who are sick or hurting may need to learn to live with a bad back, but they shouldn't have to live with our judgment. We have piled burden upon burden. Just what we all need: a double burden.

Jesus was more interested in critiquing the double burden, ones we as the church have applied generously. A disingenuous burden.

Maybe the meta-miracles experienced in the Bible were in the way that others around the woman had to change; and not just in the way they saw the healed woman but in the way they saw the men and women around them who hadn't experienced a miracle. This truly must be the miracle within the miracle. Our response. Our posture realigning.

As an individual, I have ducked and covered. As a church, we have ducked, and we have covered. As a church, we still bang away. With every resounding bang, we alienate a society craving connection; we are out of time, and the discordant notes of trust have been left on the editing-room floor.

How much better is a symphony of humanity conducted not by man's control but by God's love?

Classic Christian culture postures of "we're right and you're wrong" that end conversations are abuses of the word *conversation*. Our posture of hiddenness and entitlement, of elite tone and control, may give us the feeling of having the posture of a gladiator but is closer to the posture of a lost child, fearful that he has been left behind.

We, together, need to face the ugly truth:

Our posture is of the arrogant.
Our arrogant posture has caused so much pain.
Our arrogant posture has strangled love.
Our arrogant posture has diluted hope.
Our arrogant posture has controlled forgiveness, has trampled peace, and has crippled truth.
Our arrogant postures have chewed up and spat out trust, the giant Monty Python foot coming down heavily on an unsuspecting society.

But let us not be naive, the bus of the lost posture metaphor is full and represents everyone throughout humanity.

A humanity created gets arrogant and can't find its way back.
A business created gets arrogant and can't find its way back.
A government created gets arrogant and can't find its way back.
A church created gets arrogant and can't find its way back.
Integrity, where have you fled?
Humility, where have you hidden?
Trust, where are you hiding?

I desire to live a life worthy of a posture that has been restored by God for others—my posture, our posture, the body of Christ's posture.

The miracle of living is not found in the immediate change of posture but in the collective societal change that comes from persistent attention to our personal and collective postures toward others.

Our struggle is not with the redemption or the reconciliation; our struggle is with living a redeemed and reconciled life.

Our struggle is not so much the miracle as it is living with or without the miracle.

Paul nips this in the bud when writing to the church of Philippi, calling us to a greater humanity than a self-serving one.

> Don't push your way to the front; don't sweet-talk your way to the top. Put yourself aside, and help others get ahead. Don't be obsessed with getting your own advantage. Forget yourselves long enough to lend a helping hand.
> Think of yourselves the way Christ Jesus thought of himself. He had equal status with God but didn't think so much of himself that he had to cling to the advantages of that status no matter what. Not at all. When the time came, he set aside the privileges of deity and took on the status of a slave, became *human!*" (Philippians 2:1-8 *The Message*)

Jesus came and showed us a different way, a life and a posture lived without hesitation, without fear, and one full of trust.

Jesus got out of the buildings and onto the streets, fed the hungry, met the needs of the poor, befriended the prostitutes and broken, the elderly, the single parent, the lonely, the bullied, and he actioned hope; his posture poised for action.

Jesus, his posture;
On his knees in the garden
Brain engaged in the temple debating
Outraged at the marketplace
Jesus, his posture;
Strong in the garden, healing the "enemy"
Humble at the banquet
Patiently mentoring those around him
Jesus, his posture;
Welcoming the children
Broken at a friend's graveside
Collaborating with tax collectors and prostitutes
Jesus, his posture . . .
Disrupting the status quo
Standing defiant for the oppressed
An incarnate answer to the doubters
Arms spread wide on the cross

This is not just for biblical times. In my life my posture has evolved and devolved, it ebbs and flows more regularly than the tide; but now with my true posture found and restored. I no longer want to live hunched, slouched, ducking and covering. I want to reach.

When God intervenes, things change; lives change; the posture of history and the future changes.

Our faith cannot just be for the miracle itself but must extend beyond the miracle and into living. We can no longer live in the shadow of a miracle. Postures restored, we need to once again look up and taste the sunshine.

Six

Trust and Restoration

The Shattering
of Misrepresentation

SKY

"I hope you got this."

It was more than a statement, it was a command, maybe even closer to a desperately and squeakily voiced plea. Whatever it was, it was an understatement of epic proportions. We were ten thousand feet up over the Irish countryside, and my legs were now dangling above the clouds. I had thought this jump would be a great way to visually describe faith and trust, and in the end it was, as terror seems to be inexorably linked to honest faith, to authentic trust. But as I sat on the plane's edge, nothing but clouds below me, all I could think of was, *Olaf, I hope you got this.* Olaf was my six-foot-five-inch skydiving instructor whom I was belted to. At first it had felt just a bit too tight, but now I wanted the straps to cut off my circulation. Then he said two words, "Just breathe," and just like that we dropped into the wide air and a freedom that I suspect I will never replicate.

Trust is just a breath or a gasp away. Freedom is found in trusting.

Trust rarely seems to be serene. It's usually exhibited either in terror or in surrender. Yet, if there is one thing we should have altogether in life, it's trust. Didn't we recite this proverb when we were young?

> Trust in the LORD with all your heart and lean not on your own understanding; in all your ways acknowledge him, and he will make your paths straight. (Proverbs 3:5 NIV)

I love that "path" is plural, not some but all. Yet, as I look back at my life (and look forward to living), I see that most of my paths are crooked and wobbly like coloring outside of the lines. Maybe "straight" in the kingdom of God isn't the "straight" that we have so parochially defined. Maybe crooked is the new straight. Maybe trust is a by-product of walking *off* the radar as much as *on* the radar—maybe there is no radar with God. Maybe we have a God who is God in any weather and on any terrain. Maybe God is God no matter where I lose or find myself. Maybe trust needs different types of soil instead of one prescribed and gilded concrete.

FATHER OF STARS

One of the greatest sojourners of the crooked road of distrust was the Father of Stars. To be exact, that was the man who was promised that he would have more offspring than there were the stars in the sky. A man named Abraham.

Here are some of the highlights:

God promises children to Abraham and Sarah, a promise

that must have only felt like a dream after having waited so long.

Ten years pass. Sarah was still unable to conceive. Time has a way of weakening expected promises, and weakened promises lead us to coming up with our own solutions.

So Sarah and Abraham distrust their understanding of God's promises, scheme for results, and abuse their authority. Eventually Abraham sleeps with another woman, Sarah's maid, Hagar; and a distrust in God was not all that was conceived that day. Nine months later Ishmael is born.

They say, "the wages of sin is death," but that night we sure created new life.

—Foy Vance[1]

The pressure upon this prominent man of the time to continue his bloodline must have been intense, as well as his anger at a God who had seemingly broken a promise. A drastic and destructive choice was made.

Trust has a shelf life that expires when relationship erodes. Relationships have a shelf life that expires when trust is eroded. Trust and relationship are inextricably linked, born of the same womb.

Abraham and Sarah had limited God to their own understanding; an understandable thing to do. Yet it always leads us to forge shortcuts that turn out to be detours.

I don't want to limit God to my understanding of God. He's far grander, wiser, and more infinite than my understanding. But how often do I do that? How often do we do that? Why do we look to short-circuit trust; why do we attempt to speed up trust?

So, why was trust an issue with Abraham? God had turned up, had taken him outside and showed him the stars— the very ones the Creator had grasped and thrown into space—and had promised Abraham more children than the stars before him.

"Then he brought Abram outside and said, 'Look up at the sky and count the stars if you think you can count them.' He continued, 'This is how many children you will have'" (Genesis 15:5).

That's got to be awesome and terrifying, leading to many, many sleepless nights.

Yet, in short, they failed to trust God. But, in short, God still extends his trust toward them. What kind of God continues to trust the untrustworthy? A fool or a fanatic for love? God's faith in us is infinitely larger than our myopic particles of faith in God.

Life is a story of trust. But there will be moments of distrust like Abraham's Hagar moment lurking around every corner; personally and as a church. This is not Hagar's fault; it is wholly Abraham's—but she does represent a moment of his distrust that we can all relate to. Let's use this moment, defined by a name, as a working metaphor; what are the Hagars in our lives that we reach for or lean on, instead of persevering beyond the delayed promise? The Hagars seem like good escape hatches or get-out clauses, but there is always the small print. Terms and conditions do apply. But, shockingly and wonderfully, the Hagars still bring forth life. Our destructive choices still produce change in us, but always in hindsight and usually over time.

My chosen Hagars create a storm cloud of distrust.

MOTHER OF STARS

God then returns to the barren land and finds the barren woman by a natural spring. God then repeats his promise. This promise brings fresh water to withered hope.

"I'm going to give you a big family, children past counting."

In a beautiful boldness, "She answered GOD by name, praying to the God who spoke to her, 'You're the God who sees me! Yes! He saw me; and then I saw him!'" (Genesis 16:10, 13 *The Message*).

Distrust blinds. But we have a God who pursues clarity of sight. We have a God who sees and can be seen. We have a God who gives vision.

Think about it, God has a history of trusting the untrustworthy—us. This is humanity: on one side trustworthy and the other not so much. We kill one another, destroy the garden, call one another names, indulge, entitle, and exclude. Why trust us?

If a petulant child is consistently destructive, we put him or her in a corner. Yet God seems to have no corners. Grace has no corners. Love has no maximum capacity.

In the middle of trust and distrust, we find life; a crash-trash cocktail of a beautiful mess that we live in, a wonderful collision of hope and frustration. Yet in all we do, God is faithful beyond our detours, beyond our ill-advised, fear-derived decisions.

Fifteen years more go by. Yet time never deters a determined lover:

"The Lord was attentive to Sarah just as he had said, and the Lord carried out just what he had promised her. She became pregnant and gave birth to a son for Abraham when he was old, at the very time God had told him" (Genesis 21:1-2).

Abraham named him Isaac and was a hundred years old at the time. It wears me out just thinking about it.

Sarah said, "God has given me laughter. Everyone who hears about it will laugh with me" (Genesis 21:5-6).

God does not hesitate in restoring trust even when it speed-dates extreme distrust. God is relentless when restoring trust. And joy always accompanies restored trust. Joy is the swelling string section in the conclusion of our favorite film. But while joy is not the conclusion of trust, trust is the beginning of joy.

As God's promise to Sarah and Abraham came into its fullness, trust was restored not only to a couple but to a nation. God is in the long game. Our God is in the long game.

I understand through current and past circumstances that it's hard to trust God. The difficulty of trust is that it can't be forced; it takes history, mistakes, initiative, and commitment. Trust takes time.

This waiting and this reestablishment of trust is all pre-ambling and pre-echoing the redemption of Jesus; where trust, re-revealing itself in Jesus, reestablished a trust that was nuked in Eden and has been consistently and religiously nuked since.

It's very easy to blame "all those sinners," all those Hagars in the distrust game—as the shouting man in the room draws the most stares—but the faithful, as so clearly articulated in the Bible, are prolific in the realms of distrust. The Bible spends more time underlining the botched living of those closest to God than those seemingly far away. And so clearly exhibited to society are the ones who propagate distrust in God with such efficiency: we disobey and break God's promises regularly with a refined finesse. We've made an industry of it. A distrust behind a closed door or cloaked in tradition is no less a distrust. A slap to the face always hurts most from the ones who are closest. And the face of God is reddened and calloused from the continual collision of the churches and my arrogant displays of broken trust, our proliferation of distrust.

A CONVERSATION WITH MYSELF

As I read what I've written, I slowly begin to rock my inner child saying, *Calm down, Greg. Step down from your towering soap box. We are "real humans," mere mortals, not "Mothers and Fathers of Nations."* "Abrahams and Sarahs!" I answer myself, a bit too loudly, in a way that makes people stare, "Abraham and Sarah were human too!"

My conversation with myself continues in a self-congratulatory way, *Greg, you make a good point and I* get it. But it sounds too much like a convenient excuse to me, and one you've used before and, to our embarrassment, will use again. But then, why are you so surprised when the majority of society has no desire to set foot near a church or those who frequent it? Most of society could not care less, because they see your faith as having not cared less. Shouldn't you do something about this?

I sat with someone I hugely respect the other day, and when I challenged him on trust and future, his response was, "I don't know if I can fully trust God with my whole future." Beautifully honest. When pressed further, he expressed that it's due to the fact that he has been "let down way too much" by God's ambassadors. Tragically honest.

I get this because I am this. It's difficult to trust when we feel that God has let us down, when people let us down, when I let you down. My whole life I've attempted to trust, yet the tragedy of trust is that my life is littered with distrust.

Shouldn't we do something about that?

MRS. REPRESENT

We had had a decent service. The turnout on this Sunday morning was moderate but subdued: a mostly post-fifties congregation emphasized by the lack of, or rather the sheer absence of, kids or teenagers. The irony being that I was there to speak to the "young people," seemingly a euphemism for the absent. (In hindsight I should've given a talk to the absent ones.) Following the service, the pastor and I walked across the parish grounds for lunch. I was stopped at the threshold of the pastor's home. His wife had her arm stretched across the doorway, blocking the entrance to her home. I quickly did a recall of my sermon, wondering at which point I might have offended the most—all the while hoping to dilute and diffuse my sermon in a further hope of still getting a free lunch. Theology often falls at the feet of hunger. She looked me in the eyes, for far too long, and said, "What do we do about kids going to *that* sport on Sundays instead of coming to *our* church?" (Her emphasis.)

My stomach growling, I knew a quick answer would get me to the now-cooling roast and potatoes most expediently. So I answered, "Maybe, you could run another service later in the day or move your service to another day." (Can we now eat?)

Her answer was brisk and arresting, "It's not *our* job to change, it's *theirs* to conform." (Her emphasis. My sadness.)

My potatoes and the table discussion went cold.

RUBBISH GODS

Jesus conformed to our every whim. That's exactly what he did, right? He didn't become a man, didn't move from the temples to the beaches, didn't search for the lost. He just marinated in the distrust being propagated and waited for the hurt, the broken, the poor, and the lost to come to find him. We all know the parable of the lost sheep looking for the Shepherd, eventually finding him warming himself by the fire, feet up with the other ninety-nine and their hooves. Right?

Jesus came to shatter this misrepresentation of his Father and to restore trust. He changed his being to change our thinking.

Personally, I hate being misrepresented to others. I hate when a misrepresentation precedes me. The line "Oh, *you're* nicer than I had expected" would throw me, wondering, *What were you expecting?* Of course we project, we throw ideas and constructs and personalities and fears at others and at God; but surely that is the prerogative of those whose trust has been broken; a few should not only be allowed, they should be expected.

It's no secret that in life, trust has eroded in a fantastical fashion. Do we trust anyone or anything any longer? From movie reviews to banks and governments, to CT scans and statements, to churches and leaders—trust has been castrated. In this recession-ridden Western world, every major institution has broken the trust we have entrusted them with. Banks, government, journalism and the media, the courts, the police, and the church have all broken our trust. But we still save money, vote, watch TV, and should still pray. Hearts get broken, yet we still love. In other words, trusting at times is absolute rubbish, and it feels useless.

We may say, "How can I ever trust again?"; "They're late all the time"; "They said they'd stop drinking"; "He's ordained"; "It's my home; they said I couldn't lose it"; "They told me they wouldn't tell anyone"; "She said I was the one"; "They said it was a job for life."

Broken promises sever trust. Yet our searches for the Hagars are unquenched. Trust and distrust can always be found in close proximity.

Where in your life has trust that was frayed been restored? Or is yet to be restored? Can we recover the trust that has been broken by institutions? By others? By us?

God has promised so much, and we, the church, individuals, and society have broken the trust by looking to fulfill God's promise for us. We have sought to wrestle control of God from God and have become serial killers of trust. Society used to look at us and see God. But, having been created in God's image, we are now proficient at creating God in our own image. This is confusing to those who seek truth.

We are rubbish at being God. We've set ourselves up for this failure. The tragic result is that society has stopped looking for God in us, and for this I am thankful. Until we can humbly curate what God has entrusted, then we should be ignored.

Yet we are still relentless; we rebuild institutions instead of investing first in trust.

We create control structures to protect our truths, disconnecting and alienating others and stalling restoration.

Where have the curators of trust gone?

HOLY WATER ON TAP

If you ever come to Dublin, dig deep. Turn the corners into the alleyways, find the cobblestones and cut through the churchyards, follow the music and search for the hidden. In the midst of one of the busiest consumer byways in the capital city, you can find a tap. A twisted piece of metal sunk into a century-old brick wall. The sign above it reads

"Holy Water." It's there staring at you, offering a practical and possible beyond, dependent on either the faith or the insanity of the moment—maybe they are more closely linked than I'd like to admit.

I stood there watching this old tap one day; I watched the elderly hands of those who knew where to find the holy water—we should never stop listening to those who have lived the longest; they know where the secrets are hidden, and they only pass on wisdom to those who are listening. The cold water would splash over their hands as they attempted to fill all manner of receptacles, mostly disused water bottles and an occasional tiny glass vial—a drop of the holy being enough for the day.

I often wondered about what drove the church to put that tap there. Was it accessibility or necessity? Was it annoyance at having to dole out the water daily to a slowly diminishing crowd of those who desired it? Especially as those who wanted the water these days also wanted a lengthy conversation to go with it—surely holiness has nothing to do with the mundane nature of living or connection to the everyday. Maybe it was a desire to be environmentally friendly or maybe a desire to make it available beyond the altar.

Here we have it, holy water, on tap. A sign posted, free yet limited (9 a.m. to 5 p.m.), hidden, only for those who can find it, and controlled, having to press it every six seconds for more. Yes, this holy water tap had one of those annoying taps that only allows you to get the soap on before having to press it again, switching off just when you need it most. Ultimately, is this really a picture of grace? Why do we as the church feel the need to control everything?

Control and trust cannot coexist.

Trust is not dispensed. Trust is given.

Risking beating this poor H_2O-driven metaphor to its limits, I do wonder where these taps exist in my life, my community, my church. Taps are not just found on the walls of traditional churches. Because we are all really good at creating taps in our lives.

Taps displace trust. Limiting and controlling grace parch the soul. Cracked lips that once spoke of need now look elsewhere for satisfaction. A thirst for trust remains.

THIRST

When in doubt consult children or large animals. I love this excerpt from C. S. Lewis's *The Silver Chair*:[2]

> "Are you not thirsty?" said the Lion.
> "I'm *dying* of thirst," said Jill.
> "Then drink," said the Lion.
> "May I—could I—would you mind going away while I do?" said Jill.
> The Lion answered this only by a look and a very low growl. And as Jill gazed at its motionless bulk, she realized that she may as well have asked the whole mountain to move aside for her convenience.
> The delicious rippling noise of the stream was driving her nearly frantic.
> "Will you promise not to—do anything to me, if I do come?" said Jill.
> "I make no promise," said the Lion.
> Jill was so thirsty now that, without noticing it, she had come a step nearer.

"*Do* you eat girls?" she said.

"I have swallowed up girls and boys, women and men, kings and emperors, cities and realms," said the Lion. It didn't say this as if it were boasting, nor as if it were sorry, nor as if it were angry. It just said it.

"I daren't come and drink," said Jill.

"Then you will die of thirst," said the Lion.

"Oh dear!" said Jill, coming another step nearer. "I suppose I must go and look for another stream then."

"There is no other stream," said the Lion.

This stream is wider than the eye can see or the soul can imagine.

Let us not become those who limit ourselves, limit access or attempt to limit God's grace, hope, redemption—it is for all, especially for those who can't find it.

TREE HOUSE

We had almost finished building the ultimate tree house. It was a good twenty feet up the tree, high enough to be dangerous. It was high enough to have seen my brother fall for far too long; thankfully, he survived. It was just the perfect height. The tree house was built with the old barn's discarded wood—fastened into place, the old tree gripping back. We had the bunks and even electricity run. We even had the electric rotisserie hot dog cooker ready and waiting to sweat itself past lukewarm, making the hotdogs just about tolerable to eat. Delicious. It was the idea not the execution (or taste) that mattered. But we needed security. We cobbled together the few coins we had and set off on foot for the nearest hardware store. We knew we didn't have enough to pay for anything, but we lived in hope.

And then the miracle happened. Miracles and what constitutes miracles are in the eye of the beholder. While we were walking along the road, we came across a full wallet, jammed with cash. Dilemma. We could now afford proper security for our house in the old maple tree. But guilt bit our Sunday school–reared souls hard and left a mark— we knew we had to locate a phone (they came in large glass boxes back then) and call the gentleman who had dropped his loot. Using one of our few coins we called him. He met us at the hardware store, thanked us, and gave us $10! We were in. We spent most of it on Popsicles, got a lock, and then we walked off with a sugar high into the Michigan sun.

I held the last dollar and twisted and turned it in my hand, noticing the artwork, its design for the first time. What was that eye on top of the pyramids? Do we have pyramids in the United States? (I was a young boy.) Why haven't I visited them? Why are there so many cobwebs? Really, what's with that floating eye? And then read "In God We Trust." I hadn't seen that before. Who had written that there and why? What does that even mean on cash?

"In God We Trust," a clever turn of phrase—printed for all to see across the tops of our greenbacks; a hook-line, mantra, something to aspire to, something to question, something to betray. This phrase has extended beyond monetary value and existentially to a way of life. Yet the failing "buck" has more trust value these days than the God that adorns its text, and that's saying something.

When did God become so untrustworthy? The extensions of this query being that those who trust God are no longer trustworthy.

God's value in society is linked to our value. Our value linked to God's value. Yet I can't help feeling that God is getting the bad end of the deal. We rapidly devalue the currency of God. God is no longer worth the paper God is printed upon. Since we cannot see God physically, we are ultimately stuck with believing those who speak of following God. This inevitably leads us to failure. Because we fail.

Failure breeds distrust. Distrust gives birth to disconnect. When we distrust we disconnect, we atrophy, we begin to waste away, not only as individuals but also as a church.

What have you done, God? What did you do to deserve this? I think your fatal flaw was the crowd you chose to hang out with.

I know many will say that faith believes beyond what we can see, and of course I do believe that, but it's not the full image; it's only some of the pixels that make up the high resolution of a trustworthy relationship. The classic quote from vacation or holiday Bible camps across the globe is "You are the only Bible some people may read." We ignore this old adage at our own peril. As those of us who seek to know God are looking for a good book recommendation, an introduction, a good review. And the best review for God is you. An honest life inspires trust in he who brought life forth. We cannot let trust slowly morph into an unrecognizable friend; trust cannot become a stranger for those who seek to believe.

A lack of trust limits love.

A soul reset is needed and is only fully realized when we search for freedom and find it in the unyielding, uncontainable, uncontrollable love of Jesus—for all. The incarnate of God sought to realign the broken trust. Reset love.

Trust at its fullest allows love at its finest.

A trust restored, restores.

Seven

Trust and Faithfulness

Who Me?

COMMUNITY OF TRUST

The writer Isaiah writes: "Therefore the Lord himself will give you a sign: The virgin will conceive and give birth to a son, and will call him Immanuel," meaning God with us (Isaiah 7:14 NIV).

One of us, giving birth to God incarnate! Birth to Jesus? As a man or woman, this is terrifying. I don't care if you're a saint or a madman, if giving birth to God doesn't absolutely freak you out, then you can add delusional to your résumé.

Isaiah had prophesied this birth hundreds of years before it was fully realized. That's a lot of folks over hundreds of years walking about wondering if today was the day and if they were the ones to be chosen for the task—unenviable yet prophesied, so it was deemed important. Typical of the prophetic to not give us the specifics we need.

Then, from a seemingly simple family, we were all redeemed.

The more I read about the well-known Christmas story, the more I realize that this story is not just about the coming of a king but about us—how we respond to a call beyond ourselves, how we trust beyond a blinding fear. How the extraordinary comes from the seemingly ordinary and how in the midst of fear potential can be realized.

GENERATIONS

I sat for far too long at the children's table growing up. Relegated to a gaggle of cousins, at a fold-out table on the ugly furniture that would now adorn full-page spreads in hipster magazines; back then they were just a collection of random and busted-up chairs. Our lives had three main focuses. The first focus was do not get a single crumb on Grandma's clean floors. (We'd be charged five cents a crumb, which we'd place in the back of a worn, gray, felt, bunny rabbit bank—Grandma never really made us pay up, but threat resonates.) The second focus was to get a good slice of pumpkin pie. (To this day my grandma will make me two full pies regardless of the occasion.) And the final focus was to eavesdrop on any and every good conversation without being detected—a skill not to be underestimated. If I were at the kids' table in the house of Joseph, the story would've fueled countless post-feast conversations; the awe, the speculation, the wide eyes of disbelief, the hope for a truth.

Like all good stories, the story of Mary and Joseph would be told around the family table for generations; it's a shame they most likely would not have grasped the significance of this eternal outcome at the time. A secret, like most secrets, only revealed in time.

This is a story about people being involved, engaged, fearful, hopeful, waiting, and doing; faithful without understanding the outcomes: for this is the best kind of faithfulness. A faithfulness that incubates a trust to be needed.

So, let's have a quick look at this league of extraordinary disciples: Joseph, Mary, Elizabeth, and John the Baptist, an incredibly faithful community in waiting.

JOSEPH

A student once told me that Joseph was the Paul McGuinness of the whole Mary thing. Paul McGuinness was the very significant fifth member of U2, their manager, the person who kept the whole thing on the road in the midst of chaos and art. Joseph was much like that—not the star of the show, not out in front, but absolutely necessary.

Matthew 1:18-25 (*The Message*) reads: "The birth of Jesus took place like this. His mother, Mary, was engaged to be married to Joseph. Before they came to the marriage bed, Joseph discovered she was pregnant."

It was by the Holy Spirit, but did he know that? And continuing:

"Joseph, chagrined but noble, determined to take care of things quietly so Mary would not be disgraced."

Joseph had integrity without knowing the outcome. Trust trusts.

"While he was trying to figure a way out, he had a dream. God's angel spoke in the dream: 'Joseph, son of David, don't hesitate to get married.'" The angel spoke further—"'Mary's pregnancy is Spirit-conceived. God's Holy Spirit has made her pregnant.'"

Hold on. Let me get this clear. Joseph didn't get the heads up? He found out after she was pregnant? What could've Joseph gone through at that moment, in his head and heart? Was he a victim of a betrayed trust?

Surely it would have been better if God had sat them down together, explained it, brought in a rabbi, and married them, or at the very least, worked out the spin they would need to fabricate to keep the paparazzi away. Surely they should've built a fence before the wolves began entering the garden.

But God turned up and effectively said to Joseph, "By the way, this is happening."

How's that work with your theology?

Life is rarely judged on the situation created but more often on how we respond. Our response magnifies our character. Our depths revealed in a single moment. Does fear repel or compel? With Joseph, trust was a choice and step of faith in this intangible circumstance.

And again the reading:

> "She will bring a son to birth, and when she does, you, Joseph, will name him Jesus—'God saves'—because he will save his people from their sins." This would bring the prophet's embryonic sermon to full term [echoing Isaiah 7:14]:
>> "Watch for this—a virgin will get pregnant and bear a son;

They will name him Immanuel (Hebrew for 'God is with us.')" (Matthew 1:20-23 *The Message*)

We continue, "Then Joseph woke up. He did exactly what God's angel commanded in the dream: He married Mary. But he did not consummate the marriage until she had the baby. He named the baby Jesus" (Matthew 1:24-25 *The Message*).

Joseph did not hesitate—he got up and married her. Wow. No commitment issues there. Mary is pregnant by God, about to give birth to God, and there is no hesitation, just trust?

Would you have hesitated?

I've had plenty of wrestling, contemplating, and hesitating when I have personally chosen my future, and here we see Joseph showing such incredible obedience and faithfulness without knowing the outcome.

He had no idea how this journey was going to end for them and their family, but a preestablished trust with his God had relegated fear to the children's table, a mere five-cent crumb. Joseph didn't have centuries of hindsight to dictate "good and measured" decision-making; he only had obedience in the moment.

Joseph understood what it was to have "faithfulness before fruitfulness"[1] and how to trust the journey not the outcome. The length of time between Isaiah's prophecy and Matthew's Gospel was nearly seven hundred years. Seven hundred years of waiting. I get annoyed when my burger takes ten minutes. Trust is not time-dependent. We are called to inhabit trust, and this enables trust in others.

Joseph, in his society at the time, made some unpopular choices. But unpopular choices are the ones most likely to lead to change. We are not called to be popular; we are called to make history.

This is a micro-community whose narrative arc would come to redefine trust between God and humanity.

Faithfulness before fruitfulness.

Together let's look further at the other characters in this cast.

MARY

Silent night, Holy Night
All is calm, All is Bright
'Round yon virgin, mother and child

I used to sing these lines at the top of my voice with all my conviction focused on volume, convinced I knew the words but instead singing "Round young virgin"! At the time I had no idea what a virgin was, but I did know that round was a great description of the ladies who waddled around, me at their waist height, getting my head bumped around worse than a carnival ride.

Mary was probably fifteen, some say younger.

Mary had never had a baby.

One of most notorious verses in the Bible that captures the wrestle of both fear and trust is in Luke when the angel approached Mary and said ironically, "Do not be afraid, Mary." Uh, what?! If anyone had cause to fear it was her. If there was ever a moment to run far, far away, it was this.

But there's a gentleness that comes with the call "Do not be afraid, Mary," as the call has a name. The call of God always has a name.

Incredible that in this extraordinary situation, never to be repeated, Mary was calmed by the angel while she listened. I'd be hyperventilating, like when I was detained by Walt Disney World security. Though Mary and I are the same ages at these times, we had vastly different lives.

> She was confused by these words and wondered what kind of greeting this might be. The angel said, "Don't be afraid, Mary. God is honoring you. Look! You will conceive and give birth to a son, and you will name him Jesus. He will be great and he will be called the Son of the Most High. The Lord God will give him the throne of David his father. He will rule over Jacob's house forever, and there will be no end to his kingdom."
>
> Then Mary said to the angel, "How will this happen since I haven't had sexual relations with a man?"
>
> The angel replied, "The Holy Spirit will come over you and the power of the Most High will overshadow you. Therefore, the one who is to be born will be holy. He will be called God's Son. Look, even in her old age, your relative Elizabeth has conceived a son. This woman who was labeled 'unable to conceive' is now six months pregnant. Nothing is impossible for God."
>
> Then Mary said, "I am the Lord's servant. Let it be with me just as you have said." Then the angel left her. (Luke 1:29-38)

Mary was consumed in ways that no other human has or ever will understand. Consumed by God for us.

Mary's DNA was now mixed with the eternal; if God were to have a genetic code, then at this point it was entwined with Mary's. This blows my mind; the trust that the very Creator extended to his creation, to carry redemption in her womb, to carry the hope for the world, to carry his son. God exhibiting the desire of connectedness, restoring trust by trusting; skin and bones carrying the stardust of the omnipotent.

Often I hear in some circles the desire to suppress the role of Mary. Often I hear in other circles the desire to elevate Mary. Why do we fear this honoring of Mary? Yes, I think we need to be cautious at elevating anyone too highly, but to ignore this great disciple does a great disservice to Jesus' mother.

Mary was consumed—more so than any human being had ever been before or who will ever be again, overcome and thoroughly chosen by God for God, and thus for others. Through courage, faith, trust, and obedience she brought Jesus into the world at the age of fifteen, some say younger.

To be consumed. To be consumed at such an age, as young as my daughter's.

Let's riff on this for a couple of moments. Presumably, Mary grew up with the same expectations as her peers, those expectations possibly going unrealized; the big wedding, the stable Jewish home, maybe she wanted to go backpacking across Europe, who knows? But I don't think giving birth to the incarnate God was even in the mix.

And I wonder how the community reacted to this news? Was a there a parade thrown, a street named after her?

Was she presented with keys to the city? It's more likely that she lived in isolation; signs held high above the heads of those picketing her family home that read "slut," "whore," "get out." Did her friends distance themselves when they heard the news of her pregnancy, most likely through whispers, rumors, and gossip?

And what made Mary most suitable for such a task? Was it her ability to trust beyond the fear? Did she have the ability to listen to a life-shattering mandate without flinching, possibly with a glint in her eye? She obediently raised a child for death and resurrection, only to be left alone by her eldest son into her elderly years. Not the Hollywood ending most of us wish for.

Mary never had the luxury of reading the New Testament to see how it all works out in the end. She was there, present, in the very moments. Making choices not depending on circumstance but on trust.

I wish there was more written about Mary's life in her post-fifties. Did she become a wise mentor to the many women and men in the villages? Did she have a midlife crisis, "I've done this, now what?" Did she become a leader in the church, compelling others to live beyond themselves for others; did she become a target stalked by the fear-filled; or did she spend her early evenings on her knees in her vegetable patch silently weeping, missing the laughter and embrace of her son?

OK

I was asked the following question, "How do we know Jesus was Irish?"

The answer: "Because his mother believed her firstborn was the son of God!"

Look, most of us have been teenagers, and we may have teenagers in our homes—we all know what teenagers are like, what we were like as teens. Mary was just like us. She might have struggled with her looks, her clothes; she got frustrated with her parents, and her parents got frustrated with her. She was a teenager and although that is a modern construct, she still would've struggled with friendships, her identity, and possibly even bullying—Mary was human. She had to be tired, worn out, insecure, fearful, and unsure of her next steps. Yet chosen, she chose not to be a consumer but to be consumed by God for others.

Mary was consumed but not a consumer, the true sign of a disciple.

Faith gave her the ability to look fear in the face and to trust that it was going to be OK.
Faith gives us the ability to look fear in the face and to trust that it's going to be OK.

Trust is essential for faith. Faith is essential for trust.

Consumed by God, she magnified the love beyond the fear, and through her, Jesus would embrace humanity.

CROWNING

No one had seen God before this, and she is going to birth him, the word of her ancestors made flesh.

"No one has ever seen God, but the one and only Son, who is himself God and is in closest relationship with the Father, has made him known" (John 1:18 NIV).

I am curious about who saw the Incarnated one first. Was the midwife the first to lay eyes on God incarnate? The servant of the servant? When Mary gave birth, she probably had a midwife there with her because in the Jewish world, women would give medical care to other women. In the absence of a midwife, would Joseph have stepped up to the duties of a midwife? A lovely idea that the ostracized risk-taker could've seen the crown first. The crown describing the top of the baby's head first emerging.

Jesus the King crowning.

But Mary had nine months before the birth was to take place; she had to continue to be faithful, to have endurance in the midst of being an outcast in her own hometown.

This doesn't feel like a Wesleyan hymn; this feels more like hard work.

Sometimes life just feels a bit overwhelming, but then it comes into sharp focus, and the kingdom of God has a name, Jesus.

What God becomes, God redeems.

—Scot McKnight[2]

Faithfulness before fruitfulness.

ELIZABETH

Trust further unfolds and enfolds in the Book of Luke, chapter one. Elizabeth, Mary's cousin, had waited many years to become pregnant. She and her husband, Zechariah, recently struck dumb for his unbelief, were unable to conceive for decades. I often wonder what the world would be like if unbelief still brought with it overt signs like being struck dumb—personally, I know I would hardly be able to speak (Luke 1:5-55 *The Message*).

Elizabeth was now miraculously pregnant, the pain of years of barrenness subsiding daily as life moved the skin of her belly in waves and rolls.

How did she feel when she heard the news of Mary's pregnancy? Her cousin Mary wasn't even trying and she got pregnant. The seeming cruelty and lack of understanding of sovereignty sometimes feels far too acute.

She could've been angry, even jealous that God had easily given Mary what she had desired and waited with such difficulty for so long. Yet Elizabeth found the courage to be a true friend in the waiting. Elizabeth was found not judging, just actively waiting.

Grace is not passive.

Faithfulness before fruitfulness.

JOHN

As Mary approaches, Elizabeth's arms open wide and a song rolls in from the deep. She sings, they embrace. John the Baptist begins leaping in Elizabeth's womb, recognizing Jesus. This prophet from the wilderness was a prophet in the womb: the first to recognize Jesus would become the first to introduce Jesus' ministry to the world.

Recognizing Jesus from wombs to baptismal pools.

Recognizing God is an instinctive thing, even when we cannot fully see. Have we lost this ability, or do we just forget or fail to look?

John the Baptist would go on to preach Isaiah's passage for years to come, before Jesus appeared at the water's edge. Then John was executed before his cousin and friend, Jesus, rose again, before Isaiah's prophecies preached were fully realized.

John trusted the bigger picture even though it was yet to be defined. John trusted a legacy never to be known.

Faithfulness before fruitfulness.

Sometimes we can feel like we are just a bunch of humans in the mix—like a lost but significant fallen leaf afloat on a dark ocean's surface. But all of their lives surrounded the epicenter of the baby born to represent us all. Trust was to them extended beyond the realms of heaven to earth. Restoration has not one but many names.

JESUS

The amazing event is not that man put his foot on the moon, it's that God put his foot on the earth.

—Astronaut Hale Irwin

The Word became flesh and blood, and moved into the neighborhood.

—John 1:14 *The Message*

The author of the para-translation of the Bible, *The Message*, Eugene Peterson nails it in this verse in John. This was a mystery revealed; the words scrawled onto pages;

the words spoken in deserts and gardens; the words passed on from prophet to king; the words that had human form; the syntax now attached like sinew to the bones of a man; the words made flesh before them.

"The Word became flesh and blood, and moved into the neighborhood."

Not vice versa. There was not an expectation of the neighborhood moving into heaven.

But it wasn't easy, even for Jesus.

Jesus grew up under the shadow of the virgin's son, a boy viewed as either make-believe or a living lie, even being rejected after he later returned home. This rejection was not just reserved for the God-boy, the whole family knew this rejection—the hesitation of acceptance among their community, the looks, the glares, the words.

"He's just a carpenter—Mary's boy. We've known him since he was a kid. We know his brothers, James, Justus, Jude, and Simon, and his sisters. Who does he think he is?" (Mark 6:3 *The Message*).

The created words mocking the Word that had created them.

Faithfulness before fruitfulness.

And just like his community before him, Jesus made unpopular choices, a ministry of unpopular choices. But unpopular choices are the ones most likely to lead to change.

We are not called to be popular; we are created to live fully for others regardless of popularity. Notoriety is not a prerequisite of significance; significance is found as easily in the colors of a caterpillar's body as it is in the thin layer of gold on an astronaut's visor.

We, too, are called to faithfulness before fruitfulness. We are called forward to restore trust by trusting first, to reconnect the disconnect of God and humanity, to give a name to the nameless.

These stories articulate so much of our understanding of God and the trust he places in us. What comes into sharp focus is that the kingdom of God is personal first—it has a name, Jesus, Mary, Joseph, Alex, Jaime, Emma, Joshua, Paul, and Chloe. The kingdom of God never ceases to be personal.

Yet part of the problem with faith is it is always personal. That is why it is so intimate, so compelling, so infuriating, and so divisive. Faith is not just a concept or high ideal that we can pontificate upon and control; it is living, it is breathing, and it is personal. But personal does not mean exclusive. Faith is collective, fueled by trust.

All of their lives from Joseph to Jesus were lived for future generations. Myopic they were not. Your life lived now is for a future generation. Your legacy began before you and begins again now.

Will we be consumed by God for others?

Eight

Trust and Freedom

I Can See Clearly Now

VINYL

Ichabod, Ichabod, the glory is gone! Look, there are demons coming up from the smoke!

—David Wilkerson

I smashed a vinyl.

It was the late 1980s. It was black and yellow, and it attacked in all its spandexed glory. Stryper—a Christian glam metal band—had thoroughly arrived, throwing Bibles to/at the audiences and climbing MTV charts in very high tones—I blame the aforementioned spandex—singing "To hell with the devil." And they were casualty number one. A close second was my personal faith's innocence.

I smashed another vinyl.

The proclamations of the late David Wilkerson, a non-spandex wearing Christian evangelist, were part of a seminal moment in my understanding of the sacred and secular divide, mainly because of the repercussions that one man had on a lousy collection of albums. (In hindsight maybe he was doing me a favor.) My uncle and my mother had heard that the devil was present, and David Wilkerson had seen him dancing on the speakers of a Mylon LeFevre concert. "The beat is of the devil" was to become the verbal soundtrack to the destruction of our growing vinyl and cassette collection as well as the distraction of the "secular."

We were called to the dining room, we were asked to bring all of our albums, we were told it was time to rid ourselves of the secular, and we did so by removing Mylon, Amy Grant, Evie (really, even Evie—we can't trust Evie!— Google her and you'll see what I'm talking about; she was about as harmless as an animated ice skater), Barry Manilow, and Stryper, lifting them from their sleeves and smashing them. The carnage didn't feel like liberation or even anger; it just felt confusing. The looks on my uncle's and mom's faces were surreal as joy spread over them; the secular was exorcised from our dining room and our innocence restored. Three back-to-back seminars at our church on backward masking (where you can "hear hidden messages" when dragging the vinyl backward) trained us in how to "hear the devil in the music" and we were ready to be *in* but not *of* the "real" world.

Side note: I got great at hearing the devil—in everything; but this felt and sounded counterproductive, even at the time.

We had upgraded our soundtrack of "the beat is of the devil" to "that's not Christian; it's secular" as it was far more encompassing, far more Christian; it became the default setting for everything that wasn't what the church or my parents wanted in our lives. "We" can be trusted, but "they" cannot. "We" are sacred, and "they" are secular.

Fast-forward to seven years later when I was helping my uncle move apartments; I lifted a heavy box and curiosity got the best of me. I opened it and found The Beatles' *White Album* and Larry Norman's *So Long Ago the Garden* among many others. They had survived the sacred/secular cull. I looked at my uncle and said, "Why didn't these secular albums get broken?" His response was discombobulating, "Those aren't secular; those are classics." (I like him even more now because of his honesty.)

DEFINING THE DIVIDE

I got to digging. And in my family that meant dictionaries and *World Book* encyclopedias. They were worse for wear from residing at the base of our staircase, which was also the backstop for thousands of journeys on mattresses down the carpeted stairs and into A-Z.

I grabbed "S" and read something like this (from dictionary.com):

Secular—definition 1: of or relating to worldly things or to things that are not regarded as religious, spiritual, or sacred; temporal: secular interests.

Sacred—definition 1: devoted or dedicated to a deity or to some religious purpose; consecrated.

Years later, I learned more online from Wikipedia: "*Secular* and *secularity* derive from the Latin word *saecularis* meaning "of a generation, belonging to an age." The Christian doctrine that God exists outside time led medieval

Western culture to use *secular* to indicate separation from specifically religious affairs and involvement in temporal ones.

Although we know technically what these words mean, culturally they take on other significance. I grew up thinking sacred or Christian was inclusive and secular was exclusive and un-Godly, worldly. Now culturally—or for those "outside" the church—sacred is seen as exclusive and in many minds un-Godly, while secular just means not-Christian or just other than sacred. It seems that I grew up with a classic pre-enlightened, trust no one, frozen-in-time understanding of church and faith. And I was thawing. In my thawing I was realizing that the sacred boxes of my youth were as exclusive and even more so than those that wore the secular badge. If secular means "of the now" and sacred "dedicated to God," then I want to be a secular Christian, and I want to be a secular church of the times as well as timeless, for surely that is the God we serve and trust. I want to be dedicated to the now, but I also want to be dedicated to the eternal in the now. I want to find and serve God in both the finite and in the infinite.

I grew up hearing that God is only to be found in dusty pews as the church was the gateway to heaven, that the church was the only thing that leads us to the sacred. Effectively, that the church owns the deed to the sacred place.

But what about my home, our culture, the arts, and science—can the sacred exist here, in what I've grown to know as the "secular"? Is holy ground only found beneath those who name it holy?

Maybe the problem begins to arise when we attempt to define and separate, categorize and label, divide and control creation; when we attempt to isolate and contain God. Surely, the kingdom of God is larger than humanity's church. Why is it that relationship began in the garden, in undefined, wide-open spaces, yet we've attempted to contain it in plaster, mortar, and four walls?

SPHERES

Abraham Kuyper lived a very full life. Born in 1837 in Holland, this Dutch Calvinist theologian, scholar, and statesman grew up thinking beyond words that contain and the systems that control. Kuyper founded the Free University, wrote numerous papers, and was the prime minister of the Netherlands for four years. Faith did not bind him; Kuyper's faith was boundless.

Kuyper was a man who lived in an age of overly defined sacred and secular divides, yet Kuyper existed in the many spheres of society. Kuyper was part of the wider church that saw itself as the gatekeeper of all things sacred, and yet Kuyper was able to see the sacred beyond the church's gate. Here is a very brief glimpse of how Kuyper saw it and the parallels to today are as abundant as the rains of Ireland and continue to be as frequent.

In the medieval period, the church claimed to have the authority to give all of God's direction to all spheres. The church sat above all things and effectively controlled the moral authority over society, as they thought they *knew* God's *best*. Why do those who follow God always have the most defined God complexes?

In Richard J. Mouw's book *Abraham Kuyper: A Short and Personal Introduction*, he draws a clear picture of this disconnect; the church assumes the role of the sole distributer of God sitting atop the other spheres of life found in "state, art, economics, family, politics and science."[1] The church has become the filter of God to all of these spheres on *behalf* of God. In other words, without the church in the 1800s, God was nowhere to be seen. Society was living in a God-drought without the church to *give* them God.

Then, like a cataclysmic break in the clouds, the effects of centuries of enlightenment began to take hold. The nonreligious wanted to liberate control of their lives from the church: "If there's a God, you can have the church. We don't want or need it, especially in this controlling way." Why is it that church is more readily defined as a straitjacket than open arms?

Mouw's picture now changes, with the secularists or those of their time—the nonreligious—redrawing the landscape by placing God and the church outside of society's spheres. The church has now been regulated to the sidelines. The door to society has been locked, and church now needs to knock for entry. A fitting irony for those who allowed society's knuckles to be bloodied while banging on the door for God for far too long, the church having locked God away in its panic rooms.

We were cast from the garden, and now we are cast from society. When will we ever learn; when will I ever learn? This is no persecution, this is just stupidity—don't eat from the tree, don't attempt to control the uncontrollable God, don't exclude or divvy up and label what is in and what is out—otherwise we'll be out . . . and before you know it, we are out.

Society had kicked back, and the Western culture had reacted against the Church's attempts to exercise control over all of culture. While the medieval period may have recognized that God's role must be acknowledged, the mistake was the church's assumption in mediating that role.

Stop helping God across the road like a little old lady.

—Bono

We are not God's walking frame.

Kuyper refreshingly reimagined the picture, drawing the church as *one of the many* spheres that God alone surrounds.

> The church, then, occupies a specific sphere, an area of cultural activity that exists alongside other spheres. The Kingdom, on the other hand, encompasses the believing community in all of its complex life of participation in a variety of spheres. Wherever followers of Christ are attempting to glorify God in one or another sphere of cultural interaction, they are engaged in Kingdom activity.[2]

We can easily feel betrayed by the traditions that have continued to exercise a medieval framework in our society today. Unfortunately, we have allowed this framework to become less of a guide and more of a sledgehammer, one that breaks more than vinyls. This new violent framework distances society from a relationship with the church and indeed perceptually disconnects God from humanity.

We, the Church, have had an affair with control, and the freedom of relationship in God is tarnished, trust shattered in pieces on culture's floor. The bride of Christ is now in the naughty corner.

We don't need a new redemption, but we cry out for a new enlightenment.

The church is only part of the kingdom; the kingdom of God is bigger than the church. The church is but one of many spheres of culture, God active in all places. All spheres have a place together; all spheres are touched by grace. All spheres, all of humanity, have the kiss of the Creator upon their skin.

Sphere sovereignty says that "each cultural sphere has its own place in God's plan for the creation, and each is directly under the divine rule." . . . "*coram deo*—before the face of God."[3]

God's rule, not ours.

Are you looking in your God-given sphere and finding God? Are you choosing to participate in a work already in progress, or do you regress to the separation of God and culture, the division created by man yet restored by God? God is active already. In everything God is present. I believe that all the Creator has created can lead back to the Creator. The wood never forgets the carpenter, the canvas never forgets the artist, the heart never forgets where it found love.

RESTORATION

My ministry changed when I stopped taking God places and decided to participate in what he was already doing there when I arrived.[4]

I believe that the problem arises when we start distinguishing between what we perceive as "of God" or "not of God," sacred or secular; it is in these times that we proliferate the divide, that we infuse distrust. This is easier done than said.

Redemption and the kingdom of God are far, far, far bigger than this place, that place, or this soul's place.

Redemption erases divisions. Trust reestablishes unity.

We need restoration not amputation.

"Redemption is restoration."[5]

I AM HE

> The woman said, "Sir, I see that you are a prophet.
> Our ancestors worshipped on this mountain, but you
> and your people say that it is necessary to worship in
> Jerusalem."
> Jesus said to her, "Believe me, woman, the time
> is coming when you and your people will worship the
> Father neither on this mountain nor in Jerusalem. You
> and your people worship what you don't know; we
> worship what we know because salvation is from the
> Jews. But the time is coming—and is here!—when
> true worshippers will worship in spirit and truth. The
> Father looks for those who worship him this way. God
> is spirit, and it is necessary to worship God in spirit
> and truth."
> The woman said, "I know that the Messiah is
> coming, the one who is called the Christ. When he
> comes, he will teach everything to us."

Jesus said to her, "I Am—the one who speaks with you." (John 4:19-26)

Or from *The Message*:

"I am he," said Jesus. "You don't have to wait any longer or look any further." (John 4:26)

Everything is *coram deo*, before the face of God; whether in the mountains or in the streets, in the churches or in the clubs, it is God we seek, not a geographical place.

We cannot remove the fingerprint of the Creator from the created any more than we can remove water from water.

"There is not one square inch in the whole domain of our human existence over which Christ, who is sovereign over all, does not cry out 'Mine.'"[6]

We need to tune out the noise of control and tune in the freedom found in Christ; to see and realize the moments of grace bursting to be realized in all things and all places, influencing all spheres that we live and breathe in:

Your work
Your family
Your politics
Your art
Your money
Your science
Your church
Your community

God resonates and reverberates in the DNA of everyone, the essence of everything.

SQUINT

It was one of the most spiritual moments of my life. Revelation was ricocheting off my synapses like bodies in the pit of a rock concert. My first iPod was in hand; shockingly white, shockingly simple. Strangers wondering where I had gotten white headphones approached me; I was doing spontaneous infomercials for this new creation on buses and street corners.

It was 2001, and everything had changed. Then my iPod was stolen, and I was gutted. Version 2 came out, and I was equally gutted. What had happened to the beautiful simplicity of iPod 1? The simple scroll wheel now replaced by a series of buttons, the beauty of simplicity was corrupted. Dave Maeda of the Simplicity Consortium at the MIT Media Labs experienced the same, "They had changed something from beautifully simple to unnecessarily complex."[7]

Apple's Senior Vice President of Design, Jony Ives, then began to squint.

"The best designers in the world all squint when they look at something. They squint to see the forest from the trees—to find the right balance. Squint at the world. You will see more, by seeing less."[8]

The re-design of the iPod set in motion a Kuypernian echo in my faith journey, and that seemed to highlight the church as well. We were overthinking it.

Maybe my faith had just become way too personal and complex. My ego and identity all wrapped up in the successes of my faith or in our churches.

Maybe we're spending too much time cultivating our own trees for our own walled gardens for our own private retreats. Faith cannot be owned; it must be free in order to truly live. A good tree is a tree that shades many, that gives fruit without discrimination, that is unafraid of those who climb and play and explore every branch. Redemption is the good tree. Redemption is version 3 of the iPod and most of Jony Ives's further designs, "one image of simplicity."

I need to squint more.

3-D

I really hate those 3-D posters that are filled with seemingly random shotgun splattering of pixilated dots, a Jackson Pollock painting gone horribly wrong. But they gathered to see these images emerge.

They would say to me, "It's right there; can't you see it?"

I'd respond, "The dinosaur smoking the cigarette next to the roller skating unicorn?"

"Ahhh, no," would be their patronizing response.

Another would approach me and tell me to move my head side to side. Still I'd see nothing. Around me loads of people would be laughing and pointing and bragging about seeing this landscape or that solar system; at times I'd mimic the seers and pretend I, too, could see. Then a child approached, looked at me, and could see my lie like a neon light. She smiled, turned to the picture, stood still, and squinted. I did the same. It was when I just relaxed my eyes that the image revealed itself.

Those who follow Christ are those who walk alongside the stranger, befriend him or her, build trust, and without judgment model what it is to see, pointing to the disparate dots and enabling others to see more clearly the full picture of faith and living.

TRANSCENDENT MEDIATOR

I do believe in what the author Dean Nelson describes as the God who hides in plain sight, wide-open spaces.[9]

Whether it be Bono singing "Please" in a natural amphitheater in the countryside of England or the Northern Irish musician Foy Vance bent double looping vocals in a small club in Dublin; whether it be eating ice cream on the streets of Milan or jumping with my boys into a pool on a starry night; whether it be watching frogs fall from the sky or brothers embracing after a fight on the cinema screen; whether it be breathlessness after a long mountain hike, drenched after a cold rain shower, or standing still as the sunrise washes warmly on my face; whether it be artists like Van Gogh,[10] Banksy,[11] or comedian Tommy Tiernan;[12] whether it be silence or noise or darkness or light—there God will find me, and there I will find God. If I only look, if we only dare to squint.

Art, the transcendent mediator, and the mysteries of nature and humanity in all of its intrigues connect us to God and connect us to one another—even when we aren't looking, especially when we're not looking. It is symbiotic. Trust grows even when and where we least expect it.

Where does God find you? What inspires you? Where do you find God?

Do we dare to squint more and see the way God may see? Although God sees and knows us individually, love is indiscriminate and nothing can control it. This freedom brings reconnection. This freedom germinates trust. Trust wakes up love.

Try it, look at a crowd of people, look at a garden—now squint. We are all the same, all redeemed; no sphere of society can escape the squint-filled grace of God.

I want to be a secular-sacred Christian in a secular-sacred church, where the zeitgeist of today is in harmony with the gestalt of the eternal, where the times and the timeless coexist and inform each other of the love of Christ, restoring trust and reconnecting church and society.

BENT CARD, STICKY TAPE, AND MIRRORS

Wheeled out in their pajamas and onto the sidewalks, they emptied the psychiatric hospital. The streets around us began filling up with other Parisians and tourists all looking to the sky in the middle of the day. A group of thirty preschoolers all in uniform formed five lines of six and started to assemble something made of card. We felt like extras in a surreal Terry Gilliam film.

Out of curious fear, we asked a lady dressed for fashion and possibly love what was going on. She answered in her smooth but clipped accent "it is the eclipse, but do not look directly as it may blind you." We had no idea that there was to be an eclipse on this day, but the children, the fashionista, and the psych ward were prepared. I was gutted. I wanted to see the sun tuck itself behind the moon, the smaller moon blocking the larger star there in Paris that day.

We did see the eclipse or rather the effect of it as we turned our backs and viewed the shadows overlapping one another, disappearing and then again separating on the crowded sidewalks. A silence that was palatable in that brief moment was followed by a slight gasp, followed by laughter.

The global soul looking to the sky to see that which we could all share, not prejudiced to race, age, religion, or language. Together we enjoyed in that moment a sense of community, something beyond ourselves, greater than us but experienced by us all.

The God within is the God who surrounds.

We can choose to create with bent card, sticky tape, and mirrors, through short films or silence, through long-forgotten liturgy or lyrics, all glimpses of our collective story; we can choose to articulate that which will allow us to view the reflection of the wonder of the Creator, or we can choose to stay inside.

Nine

Trust and Being

We, the Church

BRIDE

The bride is having an identity crisis. All of her life she has dreamed of and prepared for this very moment. But now she seems to be wondering, *Is this where I'm meant to be? Is this who I'm meant to be?* The bride sits alone, locked in her room.

The guests have arrived and everyone is watching, everyone is waiting, everyone is hoping for the bride to turn the corner, to be revealed. The wait is long, some say too long. Some say the clichéd line, "good things come to those who wait." The groom shifts the weight of his standing from left to right and back again. Some of the guests have fallen asleep; some of the guests have left early, tired of the delay; frustration has set in.

Does the bride have cold feet? How long will the groom wait? How long will the guests have to wait?

The bride, an ancient term for the church, shares so many traits with brides of today and the weddings we've all been to, wonderful events laced with anticipation and tension. In this meta-narrative the waiting God plays the groom, or the bridegroom. In this scenario the church plays the role of the bride. But as we look around, the church, the bride, has a myriad of definitions, denominations, and personalities. The guests are played by those who desire to participate in the wedding, but they, we, are getting tired of the bride's identity crisis.

It takes courage to question your vows when everyone is waiting. It takes courage to realize that you may not be ready. It takes courage to change.

The church, able to speak, but with so many voices, is drowning itself out; clarity of vows is hard to distinguish, but in the midst of the noise you can hear the faint and daring questions, "Is this who I'm meant to be?"

CONFIRMATION DRESSES

Around the world, we have seasons of confirmations in both the Catholic and Anglican traditions where those being confirmed have an opportunity before God, community, family, and the bishop to say a public yes to their faith. The problem with all good traditions is that it has been hijacked by emphasizing the party and not so much the reason for the party.

The limo pulls to the front of the church steps. The chauffeur quickly exits his seat to open the door of his client. She emerges dressed in haute couture, a dress made by hand in London. Her skin is an odd shade of orange, a spray tan exposed to real sunlight. Cameras are flashing. Envelopes of cash are at the ready to be passed to her after the service. The name on the cake is obscured by a cacophony of candles. Today is her confirmation day, and this is a true story. She is eleven. Her friend had arrived by helicopter only moments earlier.

These public displays of spiritual affection (let's call them PDSAs) have grown into veritable monsters that eat the young. A competitive edge brought to the altar that wouldn't seem out of place on the catwalks of Paris.

All the good of a community surrounding her and support-ing her to go deeper in her faith is robbed by a far more shallow desire to look the part instead of being the part.

When will we stop looking the part of the church and start being the church?

BRIDE REVISITED

The bride—which, again, is the ancient term for the church—does have an identity crisis. All of its life it has been preparing for this very moment, to be the bride, to be the conduit of trust, hope, love, and relationship on behalf of God. And yet globally the church seems to be asking, "Is this who I'm meant to be?"

Do you remember this childhood rhyme? Your fingers con-torting to facilitate the hand origami:

> This is the church;
> this is the steeple;
> open the door;
> here are the people.

But my fingers would fail me, and every time I opened the church doors there wouldn't be fingers wiggling as people, just my empty palms:

> This is the church;
> this is the steeple;
> open the door;
> *where* are the people?

Obviously, I've changed the ending, but it's closer to the truth now. Too many churches are too empty. So what's going on? Where have the people gone? Where has the church gone? Does the church have cold feet? How long will God wait? His choice was made before the beginning of time. Can God regret his choices?[1]

And what happens when we find our identities solely in these institutions that have allowed themselves to erode? Do we allow ourselves to erode, as well? Or do we, feeling superior, only blame the institution? We need to acknowledge that this crisis begins in the pew; this is our identity crisis too; it does not simply and conveniently belong just to others.

A shallow identity creates a shallow faith. A heart beats beneath the surface of each one of us, yet we feel so compelled to stay on the surface of the skin. Is it that we fear what lies beneath, as a person, as a church?

Maybe too much time has been spent preparing the surface instead of just doing. Dressing up the building instead of going outside of it to find the guests and the groom.

BELCOO

President Obama and many other world leaders were coming to town for the G8 Summit in the middle of the recession, and we were spending hundreds of thousands of pounds giving the town some architectural Botox, more than one hundred buildings being Disney-fied.

The *Irish Times* reported,

> In the one-street town of Belcoo, the changes are merely cosmetic. At a former butcher's shop, stickers applied to the windows show a packed meat counter and give the impression that business is booming.
> Across the street, another empty unit has been given a makeover to look like a thriving office supply shop. Locals are unimpressed.
> "The shop fronts are cosmetic surgery for serious wounds. They are looking after the banks instead of saving good businesses," said Kevin Maguire, 62, an unemployed man who has lived all his life in Belcoo.[2]
>
> Phil Flanagan, a relative of the former owner of Belcoo's butcher shop, says: ". . . It's a huge lie and a false economy."[3]

You can almost hear the unimpressed folks of Belcoo saying, "Are you serious? What a waste of money; they should use it for something that benefits the community. These shops are nothing but a facade, a thin veneer, a shop front with nothing going on but words and images. This pageantry is just a flagrant disregard for the real needs mocked by sticky tape and plastic bread."

Trust in the institution of the government to reach the real needs of Belcoo had been severed with a disparaging

flare. A severed trust is an artery in need of open-heart surgery. The institution's fraudulent, detached self had been
exposed.

"The shop fronts are cosmetic surgery for serious
wounds."

These are dangerous echoes in the church today. Have we,
the Church, become the G8 Belcoo butcher shops of the
world? The bride is beautiful, but her tear-streaked makeup
has carved grooves into her integrity. What have we
become? Is this where we are meant to be as the bride of
Christ? When a bride becomes a machine, the heart must
be searched for again.

The bride is on a life-support of grace, and we, the institutions, have managed to pull the plug on trust in today's
society. The Church was never meant to be the patient; the
church is the hospital and the neighbor with a warm meal
to welcome you home.

We can no longer be the sleeping church with just a false
or insular storefront of activity—the windows jammed with
dusty trinkets, glow-in-the-dark rosaries, or Facebook likes.

BREAD

I went to squeeze the bread as I had my whole life, looking
for freshness in the Wonder Bread that I remembered as a
child, an inadvertent reflex. But this wasn't West Michigan;
this was Western Europe. The church was over a thousand years old, and its shelves were stacked with at least
twenty fresh loaves of bakery bread—no brand names,
handmade. But when I squeezed the loaf it was solid, hard

as a rock. Puzzled, I asked the curate, why there was stale bread on the church's shelves. He explained that centuries ago they had been given a grant from a wealthy land-owner to give food to the poor and the poor no longer come, so we no longer buy fresh bread. We keep it here as a reminder of the landowner's generosity.

My mind was spinning. I was left wondering if the rea-son the poor no longer come is that they had to find the church, walk the length of the aisle, climb over the gilded gate, and reach up to get the bread. And having traversed this gauntlet, they found stale bread. You only have to taste spoiled milk once. Opportunities lost and trust ex-acerbated for the cost of a loaf of bread. A loaf of stone given when bread was asked for.

Why do we insist on keeping the past around just to re-mind us of a generosity that no longer affects our present? This is just an abusive delusion: "Oh, look at us. We were so good back then."

Generosity unresolved is a mockery.

That hard bread should be taken down and passed around the church congregation, allowing an embarrassment, guilt, and conviction to rattle us beyond the papier-mâché identities that we have created. We, the Church, can no longer sleep behind closed doors, spooning the poor's stale loaves of handmade bread.

A good friend of mine once struck me speechless when he said, "We killed Jesus, but the church killed God."

God cannot be killed, but we, the Church, seem to have become so immersed in becoming a successful institution that we've forgotten who it was we were meant to be all along. We are suffocating under the weight of perception and control, buried in stale bread.

This is the common, if not fully articulated, understanding of our current standing. And we have to do something about this.

We, the Church, need to become again places of healing for serious wounds, wounds that we need to openly admit to having inflicted. We can no longer be silhouettes of shame. We need to be fully engaged in being hope, rebuilding the Church from the decline up.

We, the people, need to be fully engaged in the reimagining of the body of Christ, as the true Bride, and become the restorers of trust to the groom, Christ. We are here. We are ready. The wait has ended.

We, as a Church, need to move from being a question about love to being a declaration of love.

We are born entrepreneurs of a love that is unrestrained.

THE WHY

One of the most profound Ted Talks I've seen is Simon Sinek's "Start with Why." I highly recommend you stop reading now and watch it. Here's an excerpt:

> But very, very few people or organizations know why they do what they do. And by *why* I don't mean "to make a profit." That's a result. . . . By *why*, I mean: What's your purpose? What's your cause? What's your belief? Why does your organization exist? . . . And

why should anyone care? Well, as a result, the way we think, the way we act, the way we communicate is from the outside in. . . . We go from the clearest thing to the fuzziest thing. But the inspired leaders and the inspired organizations . . . all think, act, and communicate from the inside out.[4]

For the church, our "inside" is a concerted effort to connect with the Creator and live from that place outward. Prayer is recognition of reality.

WEDDING CAKE

The wedding cake wobbled. Not a good sign. She was in her eighties, it was the 1990s, and we were in our twenties. The cake was precariously balanced on two weathered hands, and the walk up the aisle took ages.

Prague is a stunningly beautiful city. The city had been suffocated by communism for decades, but faith refused to be. We were running a youth event, and hundreds had arrived to the old, beautiful, worn Catholic church sitting on a small hill above the city. We laughed, sang, prayed, and spent hours outside in the grass with the teenagers and their families, using our broken language to find commonality.

Then a cake.

The old woman sat down on the old pew at the front of the church with the cake in her lap and smiled gently. I walked over and, with the help of a translator, chatted with her. She spoke of a childhood of poverty during the formation of her country; she spoke of World War II; she spoke of communism; she spoke of springtime and voting and the baking of a cake.

I had almost forgotten the cake—but who can ever forget a cake, especially a wobbly, delicious one? She told me that she had prayed for decades for their young people to come to know God. And we were finally here. We were the answer to her decades of prayer. She cried as she spoke. I cried as I listened.

The beauty of this humble, strong woman revealed decades of questioning governments and God—I wonder if she ever wondered, *Is this where I am meant to be?*—but that questioning had turned to prayer and that prayer to a living change.

The cake tasted of plums and poppy seeds. It tasted of long-awaited joy. It celebrated the return of the guests to the wedding, the return of the bride to the ceremony.

The Church, the bride, has gotten dusty with inertia, but I've seen old brides dance, and it's a beautiful thing.

LIVE FROM THE "WHY"

While what you do changes, why you do remains.
—Cameron Stewart[5]

We need to live from who we are, giving from the *why* and the *what* we have, not apathetically sitting back and waiting for it to happen but engaging, tuned into God. With an ear to heaven and with the eyes of eternity, we will change, and so will the lives around us.

Trust restores trust.

Simon Sinek encapsulated it when he says, "People don't buy what you do; they buy why you do it."

When we authentically give of *what* we have, from *who* we are, understanding our *why*, then revelations are found, and these revelations lead to unexpected revolutions in our homes, workplaces, communities, and churches. Trust is truly restored when we give without knowing the outcome.

Again, because we know who we are and why we are, it doesn't matter where we are. Because we are where God dwells.

You are exactly where you are. Embrace it. See change.

This passion for living, this knowing, has been placed deep within each one of us, a soul tattoo that resonates. If we stop long enough to listen, we can a find deeper understanding of who we are, why we are, and ultimately who God is, as well as where we are meant to be. Your soul is "a thousand beacons going out begging you to soar."[6]

Trust runs down the aisles gathering its guests and embracing the future.

Ten

Trust and Peace

The Abnormality of Beauty

SLOW DANCE

For me, reading the Bible at times is like the slow dance
I had at age eleven with my third stepmother at a family
reunion. Awkward. Foreign. Slow. While it was necessary, it
also felt like it would never end. She and it—the Bible that
is—were part of the family. You may not be shocked to
find out that my third stepmom (homemade ketchup and
canned tuna soup aside) turned out to be a good addition
to my life at times, though I didn't understand it at the
time; and so did the Bible, at times, though I didn't understand it at the time.

Maybe the scriptural awkwardness that grew throughout
my childhood years was due to my experience of the Bible
being punctuated by two distinct associations: victory and
defeat.

On the victory side of things, there was the celebrated
Sunday school game of the ages: Bible Sword Drill. God's
word is the "sword of the Spirit," you know. In Sword

Drills, we kids sat in a row, massive "genuine leather" King James Versions in hand—*our swords*—and our bodies poised for the hunt. The Hunger Games at Grace Bible Church. The Sunday school teacher shouted out the reference for a verse, and with reputations on the line, we raced to find it. Sword Drills served to establish the obvious and inseparable connection in my mind between God, weapons, and winning.[1]

Standing next to me in the only church service he and I ever attended together, my first dad said to me, "I don't get it. I thought Jesus was a pacifist."

I was a kick-ass Bible Sword Driller and won numerous medals at my church. I'm sure this helped me to overdevelop a sense of reward-driven spirituality. *I won! So this means Jesus loves me even more, right?* What a prize!

My understanding of the Bible as an agent of defeat came when my mother, exhausted by annoying children, shouted: "Gregory, go to your room and read the third chapter of James . . . now!" I still shudder when the Book of James pops up in the liturgy. This, in fairness, was usually because I had driven my mother to distraction through my own cheek and provocation, and she felt that some solid biblical truth would get me back on track. (That and making me literally chew on some Irish Spring soap. Oh, the irony that I now live in Ireland!)

PEACE

Victory and defeat, they sing such a strange disharmony, leaving me without peace. It's difficult as a kid and as an adult to find peace or to trust in the Bible or its ghost writer (the Holy Ghost . . . see what I did there?) when its perceived purpose seems to be to control others by winning. It feels like a strange reason for this book to exist; its perceived purpose to prove who's right and who's wrong. A weapon for winning.

Maybe it is usurped authority that we wield as our own that is in part to blame. Maybe the Gonzo journalistic artist and Hunter S. Thompson collaborator, Ralph Steadman, was right when he said, "Authority is the mask of violence."[2]

But God's word is not a weapon, and our genesis is not for killing but for creating only.

You can imagine my recent surprise when, a few decades after my stunningly awkward slow dance, I opened the Bible and found Saint John and Saint Eugene (Peterson) metaphorically tapping the stethoscope on my bare chest, telling me to breathe deeply. I paused. I took a breath, and the verses I inhaled spoke of "peace" and "don't be distraught."

"That's my parting gift to you. Peace. I don't leave you the way you're used to being left—feeling abandoned, bereft. So don't be upset. Don't be distraught. . . . Get up. Let's go. It's time to leave here" (John 14:25-27, 31 *The Message*).

Those words grabbed me and shook my bones. They first hit me in that unavoidable and frustratingly self-centered way. I felt the words vibrate from within my own story. But more than that, I felt those words ricochet throughout *our* story; not just the church as the body of Christ but throughout the global soul. This is Our Story. The story of a tangible, God-given peace that is found both in the bright dawn and in the dark storms of life. This book is a document of freedom.

FRAGMENTS

To know me is to know my dysfunction.

My soul has a scar, and its name is "Forgotten." The feeling that I don't belong has been a resounding, trust-absent, peace-barren echo in my guts since childhood. This scar gets fainter as I get older, but it's texture all the same. My struggle with peace, at times of biblical proportions, is evidently not just a biblical problem; it's very personal.

My scar whispers—and sometimes shouts—about my broken family. It speaks of the brokenness of some of the churches I've attended. My scar sometimes aches with the confusion of attending multiple schools, living in many homes, having fragmented friendships, and having a battered faith in God.

And all these fragments are as scattered across the globe as I have been—a person who has lived abroad for most of my life.

I am very thankful that I grew up knowing that there was beauty to be found in these fragments, these broken things. I may wish to trade a few parts of my childhood, but I would never trade the distinct whole, the broken spectrum of my childhood, which still refracts light. My story has given me many a wonder, but lumped in with it was the accelerant of feeling abandoned and forgotten amid a myriad of broken promises.

Broken promises are like weak tree branches; you can't trust them, and there's no peace in the climbing. So when the Book of John has the audacity to tell me not to feel upset or distraught but to be at peace, it rattles me to the core in unexpected ways. Anger and hope are now on the dance floor in that awkward slow dance.

Yet I want this peace. I crave it. But peace is elusive.

Then Jesus makes a promise, "That's my parting gift to you. Peace. I don't leave you the way you're used to being left—feeling abandoned, bereft. So don't be upset. Don't be distraught . . . Get up. Let's go. It's time to leave here."

Together.

God never promised it'd be easy, just that we wouldn't be alone.

FLESH AND BLOOD

What I'm constantly amazed at is that even those closest to Jesus struggled with knowing peace even though they had felt his calloused hands on their shoulders, his breath on their faces, the stench of his sweat in their noses, and they knew the sound of his laughter. He was present with them. Peace had a name: *Jesus*.

Presence precedes peace.

> *The Word became flesh and blood,*
> *   and moved into the neighborhood.*
> *We saw the glory with our own eyes,*
> *   the one-of-a-kind glory,*
> *   like Father, like Son,*

Generous inside and out,
*   true from start to finish. (John 1:14 The*
*   Message)*

His peace was not—*is* not—a whisper from the dead. It is not a postcard sent from the road, a support check slipped under the door in silence. It is physical. It is tangible. This is the very Jesus saying: I'm here, and I get it. My immortal *physicality* impacts your mortal *fragility*. I'm not a leaver and I'm not a hand-holder, so here is a parting gift, "a comforter" (KJV): "You know him already because he has been staying with you, and will even be in you!" (John 14:15–17 *The Message*).

Here is peace. Peace be with you. A piece of myself I give to you. Only this kind of peace can penetrate the skin and the soul and can touch the loneliness in the human condition.

Jesus, a piece of you enables a peace in me.[3]

PRESIDENTIAL INAUGURATION

Yet peace has a way of evading us even when we are representing it.

It's November 11, 2011, and Dublin Castle is filled with dignitaries and me. It's as surreal as it sounds. Michael D. Higgins is about to be inaugurated as the Republic of Ireland's eleventh president.

My job was basic: don't muck up the peace, literally. I was one of ten to pray the beatitudes as part of the service; my lines, from Matthew 5:9 (NKJV), "Blessed are the peacemakers, for they shall be called sons [and daughters] of God."

On national television it looks so sedate; the reality was that it was a major honor wrapped in a chaotic riot to proclaim and project peace to the thousand assembled and the millions watching.

In hindsight I see that that is a far more accurate portrayal of peace than a whispered prayer. We don't need to feel peace to know peace.

A PROBLEM WITH STEEPLES

Here's my problem: I love and am a part of the body of Christ, but the peace I find in it today seems evasive, elusive, and exclusive, not like the Jesus I've read about and experienced.

People don't turn up where there isn't peace, and the church doesn't have a great record of showing it, so why would they bother? I can understand why people don't "claim" church as their own anymore. When many did, it burned them or people they love. It may have created too much grief, and they may just be sick of the pain.

When the church is not at peace with itself, it cannot show peace. And we are the church.

Steeples, which could serve as lighthouses to guide us home, now rise up like jagged middle fingers to a society that needs beacons of peace. Yet the actual presence of peace has eroded in the tides of entitlement. Peace is not exclusive.

My daughter once said, "Church can't just be for the people who can find it." Surely, more than those who enter a church are in need of peace, right? Are we now actively avoiding the places that are in need of peace?

This peace that Jesus left behind, having affected individuals and nations, has now breathed a collective sigh, seemingly giving up, now failing to penetrate the fear, the distrust, the hurt that we have caused in our exclusivity. Peace has become a plastic sword on dragon skin—blunt, ineffective. A punch line in an ill-timed gag.

This is a far cry from "Peace. I don't leave you the way you're used to being left—feeling abandoned, bereft."[4]

ENCHILADAS

Reportedly, Woody Allen once said something along the lines of, "Eighty percent of living is just showing up." Recently in our family, we have been feeling rattled. It was family stuff, work stuff, life stuff. A sudden family illness. A violent burglary. A confusing transition in work. The old demons of abandonment reared their familiar heads in my mind.

Then a friend showed up at our door with freshly made enchiladas. It was simple: simple enough to change our posture that day and that week. Sometimes, it's just that simple. Peace follows presence. A piece of you always precedes a peace in me.

Why are the seemingly simple things—like accepting comfort or giving hope—so difficult?

It's all about the enchiladas.[5]

THE ABNORMALITY OF BEAUTY

Globally, the phrase "Peace be with you" resonates with us. In traditional churches in Ireland, we used to cross the aisles to reach out and sometimes even embrace one another, saying, "Peace be with you" in every mass. Lately, though, it feels like we are increasingly concerned with personal space, cleanliness, and not too much contact. We keep the holy water beside the hand sanitizer and stay on our side of the aisle.

But when we let it, peace can be wonderfully disruptive. I went to mass on a Tuesday in the Wicklow Mountains, and it changed everything for me. It was there, in a battered church with its scar-faced priest, that verses about peace moved beyond syntax and began to shape me. The normally mundane became abnormally beautiful.

At the sign of peace, the priest walked up and down the church, pew by pew, shaking the hand of everyone in the building. Even the hard-to-reach ones. Especially the hard-to-reach ones. A mother who had lost a son in a car accident, looking grief-worn, possibly questioning the cruelty of sovereignty. Two men who chose not to receive the Eucharist. A silent Protestant at the back. And all the other outsiders, muddied by the day and its rain. All were welcomed and offered peace by this abnormal priest in a battered church. This priest found his destiny in being a restorer of trust between God and us. A restorer of trust between us and us.

Peace is a refraction of trust.

This priest's authentic faith began to restore dignity and care to a broken church and broken people. I pray that abnormalities like this continue to cross aisles and walk out of the buildings, offering restoration to all. The priest could have retreated and entrenched himself in the safety of the altar, but by understanding his own brokenness, he was able to break through, reaching out to embrace the brokenness in the room.

I want to be that guy.

I want that to be my church.

What if, in those moments of giving the sign of peace, we choose to move beyond words and into action? What if we say that peace is, effectively, me giving a piece of myself to you? That is Jesus' way: I'll be there for you beyond words and with my whole being. Here's my money, my time, my car, my home, my all. And not just when it's convenient.[6]

Love is not convenient. Whenever we actively choose to give ourselves away, we create life. Where we are indifferent, atrophy prevails. A piece of my life I give to you, that you may know true peace.

Mother Teresa said, "Love to be real, it must cost—it must hurt—it must empty us of self."

Easy for her to say, she's Mother Teresa. But she wasn't always Mother Teresa; she was once just Anjezë Gonxhe Bojaxhiu. The same Holy Spirit that rattled and lived within her resides in us. There are no superior or inferior brands of the Holy Spirit, based on birthright or socioeconomic status.

The difference is in the way we choose to respond.

Mother Teresa—Anjezë Gonxhe Bojaxhiu—chose to follow the Holy Spirit, unreservedly.

Peace follows presence.

DIRTY CHURCH

You and I can be the restorers of peace.

Peace can be found when we get stuck with our hands deep in the soil, muddied in the beautiful muck of life. Maybe there we can become a dirty church of peace shaped by God incarnate, Jesus, whose hands were in the sand, who spit in the mud, who was cut and bruised by the weight of the cross.

Jesus cried at his friend's tomb.
It is his blanket that covers the homeless.
It is his hoarse voice that calls for peace.
It is his heart that breaks over the abuse of a child.
His body is hunched over a child ripped apart by a land-
    mine.
His arms are wrapped around the mother who cries alone.
His hands are pulling the plug of the electrified chair.
His front door is thrown wide open to the lonely.
His love and peace are offered unconditionally, to
    everyone.

Jesus became human, was blessed, broken, and was given for us.

My soul's determined exhalation is

Take me.
Bless me.
Break me.
Give me to others.

My awkward dance with Scripture and in life continues. But the Bible is not a weapon, a gag, an electric chair, a

Xanax, a pacifier, a slogan, or an excuse—it is freedom personified.

These days I'm a little more sure-footed with the knowledge that I no longer dance alone, that Jesus has left me his extraordinary and tangible partner in peace.

Piece be with you.

Eleven

Trust and Hope

Embracing Our True Selves

MY BODY FOR WATER

I woke with a start, my voice aching and hoarse from a sleepless night of shouting at the stars, more so at the Creator whose hands "flung stars into space."[1] My mind had been on a consistent feedback loop as I tossed and turned on the wooden floor of the orphanage we were staying in—the words "this is not right" flashing like a neon sign.

I was asked, at the age of fifteen, to travel to Mexico on a short-term mission trip to work with disadvantaged kids in this very underdeveloped village.

There was a small river running through the shantytown. That river was the place where their "toilets" drained, their animals died, their clothes were washed, and where they got their drinking water.

One evening, while hanging out on the banks of this slightly flowing sewer, playing with children, a young girl of thirteen approached me. Now, all of us have been or will be thirteen. We all know thirteen-year-old girls; some of us have them for sisters, daughters, or friends. This thirteen-year-old came up to me and, through a translator, solicited me for prostitution. She wanted to sleep with me for money.

I was fifteen, from a safe middle-class neighborhood in the United States. I had never spoken to a prostitute, let alone one so young. Geneva still a lifetime away, I was stunned and didn't know what to say. Finally, I dug deep and got the courage to just say, "Why . . . why are you doing this?"

Through the translator she spoke, "My father left my mother and two sisters when we were young; this is the only way for me to make money for clean water and a bit of food."

What would you say in this situation; what would you do? I thought of my life and realized that even in my darkest times as a mere fifteen-year-old, of feeling alone, being from a broken family, being bullied, angry or unforgiving, that I always, deep down, knew there was hope to be found. Shell-shocked I said, "But there is hope."

She looked back at me and said four words I will never forget, "There is no hope."

There is no hope.

I was floored, the wind taken right out of me, and I just stared. She quietly walked away. And I continued to stare at the space that this young girl had once occupied. There is no hope.

That night I went back to the compound we were staying in to protect us from the poor, and I went to the top of a small hill and shouted, screamed, raged at God until my voice was hoarse. My many four-word sentences echoing into the compound, "This is not right. This is not fair. Where are you, God? How can there be thirteen-year-old prostitutes saying, 'There is no hope'? How can there be thirteen-year-old prostitutes? Where is the hope?"

And just then in the silence after my storm, I felt as if God slowly reached down and woke me from my sleep, like a parent comforting a child who has woken from a nightmare, whispering words that formed ideas that shook and compelled me: "You are the hope, you must be the hope."

Not just me, I don't have a messianic complex, but this was the moment I woke up to the world beyond Greg, where I understood the eternal punch line. We must be hope to others.

"Don't think you have to put on a fund-raising campaign before you start. You don't need a lot of equipment. *You* are the equipment" (Matthew 10:9-10 *The Message*).

A year later I left home, and I have spent my life searching for and attempting to inspire hope in others.

I do look back and wish I had actually raised some money and helped that young girl and family out. But I didn't, and this is a regret I carry, a regret that I've gotten good at ignoring. But that moment is never far from me—although that's easy for me to say as a middle-class kid who can escape poverty and who will never need to trade his body for water. Yet it still does wake me from apathy when I feel like there is no more I can do or when I'm soaking in my laziness, my good intentions wasted, and drooling on a half-eaten pack of Pringles. Wake up, Greg, hope is needed.

"You will always have the poor among you" (John 12:8). It's a reality that shouldn't be. But the only people who continually say it are beauty queens in their speeches: "I want world peace and to end hunger." I may have not understood generosity at that age and maybe I was incapable of such generosity at the time, but hindsight cannot be an excuse or a reason to stop reacting to need. But my life tends to be spent with the pins and needles of a deep sleep in my arms and legs—numb and unable to reach toward or lift others out of trouble.

I often hear the classic "Jesus is the answer." But Jesus is not the answer to everything. If someone is hungry, telling them Jesus loves them is not the answer; food is.

If someone can't afford their electricity bill and will lose power, telling them Jesus loves them is not the answer; taking money out of our pockets is.

If someone is crying over the death of a friend, telling them Jesus loves them is not the answer; a silent, long, and consistent embrace is.

Jesus is not the answer to everything. (At the same time I'm tired of not saying Jesus, when I mean Jesus; this is a paradoxology that I wrestle with often. We can neither fear speaking Jesus' name nor fear not speaking it.)

Again, Jesus is not the answer to everything. Living our lives for others like Jesus is.

NEW TRICKS

In San Francisco at St. Boniface's Catholic Church, they have made a use for their church found empty on the other six days of the week, or what most of us call life.

They "let the homeless of their city sleep in the pews."

"Every weekday the program uses the sanctuary's rear 76 pews between 6 a.m. and 1 p.m. while providing access to the church's amenities like bathrooms, blankets, clothing vouchers and haircuts, executive director Laura Slattery told the Huffington Post in an email."

She continues, "This sends a powerful message to our unhoused neighbors—they are in essence part of the community, not to be kicked out when those with homes come in to worship."[2]

Gulp.

They are "not to be kicked out when those with homes come in to worship."

After Retweeting this article a friend responded, "Homeless people, in addition to needing housing, have primary needs of calm, safety, beauty, and a sense of belonging." And asked, "How can the church provide?"

I responded: "I don't think we have a choice. Either we try or we close our doors."

Another interjected, "Wow, can you imagine the day the church is seen as 'dirty' because it loves the 'least of these'?"

I added, "This is my new goal, tagline, and raison d'être, to raise up a 'Dirty Church'!"

At the entrance of my shared offices in Christ Church Cathedral, Dublin, they recently installed the stunning seven-foot-tall sculpture, *Homeless Jesus* by Tim Schmalz; Jesus is covered by a blanket sleeping rough, only the holes of his feet giving away his scarred glory. My hope is that becomes a signpost for a place of rest and not just another inspirational monument.

PAJAMAS

Every Sunday just before lunch, the community would awake and emerge from their homes and hang out in their front gardens chatting and welcoming the day with the neighbors. This neighborhood was working class or used to be before the recession; now they too were wresting the corpse of the Celtic Tiger—a six-year period in the Irish economy where disposable income and shopping in New York at Christmas seemed to have become the "norm." As they walked up the roads to grab bread, eggs, and rashers for a morning "fry" (sausages, bacon, eggs, beans, black and white pudding, and toast), their pajamas would stir no reaction. It was Sunday, and today this is our neighborhood's national dress. It spoke of a comfort with one another.

In the midst of this small town in the middle of a thriving metropolis stood a small church. It was perfectly placed to participate in this community to give to the evident areas of need that existed in the cracked homes and faces of those who understood what it was to survive tough times; "tough times" is not a euphemism but a hard-fought reality.

We approached the local pastor and asked if we could come and work within the community with the church, wondering who in the area he was friends with that we could connect with, maybe run something just before lunch on a Sunday, a pajama party?

The pastor's terse response was immediate, like a reaction more than a reply, "That'll never work as our service is at 9 a.m."

I asked, "Could we move the service back and invite the community?"

Pastor: "NO. We get in, do our service, and get out before the locals wake."

The pastor's church had moved to the suburbs, but the congregants were commuting back to the church of their childhood; the church of yesterday was oil to the water of the new local community, and the pastor didn't want to mix, let alone serve one another.

Songwriter Keith Green sang it with cutting clarity, "The world is sleeping in the dark, that the church just can't fight, 'cause it's asleep in the light."[3]

Wake up sleeping, entrenched church so that together we may go and welcome all to our beauty-drenched, dirty church.

"Where you invest your love, you invest your life. . . . Awake my soul."[4]

Trust finds traction in the dawn of an awakened soul.

OLD DOGS

Together let's travel back to the garden of awakened souls.

> Then Jesus went with them to a garden called Geth-
> semane and told his disciples, "Stay here while I go
> over there and pray." Taking along Peter and the
> two sons of Zebedee, he plunged into an agonizing
> sorrow. Then he said, "This sorrow is crushing my life
> out. Stay here and keep vigil with me."
>
> Going a little ahead, he fell on his face, praying,
> "My Father, if there is any way, get me out of this. But
> please, not what I want. You, what do *you* want?"
>
> When he came back to his disciples, he found
> them sound asleep. He said to Peter, "Can't you
> stick it out with me a single hour? Stay alert; be in
> prayer so you don't wander into temptation without
> even knowing you're in danger. There is a part of you
> that is eager, ready for anything in God. But there's
> another part that's as lazy as an old dog sleeping by
> the fire.
>
> He then left them a second time. Again he prayed,
> "My Father, if there is no other way than this, drinking
> this cup to the dregs, I'm ready. Do it your way."
>
> When he came back, he again found them sound
> asleep. They simply couldn't keep their eyes open. This
> time he let them sleep on, and went back a third time
> to pray, going over the same ground one last time.
>
> When he came back the next time, he said, "Are
> you going to sleep on and make a night of it? My time
> is up, the Son of Man is about to be handed over to
> the hands of sinners. Get up! Let's get going!" (Mat-
> thew 26:36-46 *The Message*)

Jesus goes to pray. He asks his friends to stay awake and
support him, to follow through on a simple request, but

they sleep. There is no doubt they were tired from the journey, the week that was in it, but this is Jesus on the verge of death—and they take a nap. I wonder, does this speak of confidence or complacency? Jesus has to wake them time and time again. His soul crushing under the weight of the future, his desire to journey together even in the darkest hours, his desire to be in community even when he is at his lowest, compels Jesus to walk around waking his friends; let's not do this alone, this isn't a one-man show, and it will never be.

The disciples' good intentions are just a fleeting dream. Trust was dormant on the garden floor.

But Jesus is in the waking-up business. Jesus inspires, incites, compels, and encourages us to live wide awake. And we, like the disciples, need it; for where we lack encouragement, we entertain apathy.

Still, at another time, Jesus lets them sleep on; how many of us have been left to sleep on? Have we the church been left to sleep on?

I used to wake up from my afternoon naps hearing my brothers and my friends playing in the back yard, and no one had woke me! The feeling of missing out was visceral. Yet in life it has become so easy to nap in the presence of need, in the presence of a King in need. I want to be awakened. I don't want to sleep in the presence of need.

What did they miss when they were asleep; God's son is weeping, vulnerable and intimate, but still determined and obedient? What an astounding sight that would have been to behold; respect, trust, and truth solidifying in the beauty of brokenness.

What do we miss when we are asleep?

Wake up, sleeping disciples. Wake up, sleeping Greg.

I think Isaiah says it best; "So wake up! Rub the sleep from your eyes! Up on your feet" (51:17 *The Message*).

At times, I can see us getting excited at the beginning of ministries alongside the disciples saying, "Come on everybody let's go and heal, cast out demons, feed the hungry, care for the broken." But quickly that becomes, "I'm just gonna lie down here and take a nap; let's not be so quick to get off this mountain; let's build an altar here to remember the great sleep we had; let's write some liturgy and songs and gather and sing about this sleep; by the way, Jesus, thank you for calling me—it feels great—but I'm good here."

Or maybe we just take a leisurely walk basking in the "call" to follow, walking away from Jesus instead of with Jesus. Full of ourselves, have we left Jesus behind us?

Sleeping disciples, surely it is time for us to come down from our mountains and get stuck into the streets that surround us. Down from the safety of our gardens and into the city square. Society sees the weary steeple-topped buildings and our branding, yet the church is in a deep sleep.

Meanwhile Jesus heals and weeps and laughs and celebrates and carries a cross through the gutters of our living.

Life is not just about being called like the disciples; like you and I, it is about staying alert, having eternity's eyes.

Redemption wakes us from our slumber and compels us to participate in the restoration of lives. Redemption leans in and compels us beyond our sleepwalking.

Restoring trust is about staying awake.

Jesus didn't talk about love—he loved.
Jesus didn't talk about friendship—he was a friend.
Jesus didn't talk about forgiveness—he forgave.
Jesus didn't talk about discipline—he actioned it.
Jesus didn't talk about death and resurrection—he died and rose.
Jesus didn't talk about redemption—he redeemed.
Jesus didn't threaten to come to earth and walk among us—he did it.
Jesus didn't just talk about it. He did it.

Trust ultimately comes down to two words: "follow through."

Good intentions are just cruel intentions if they are not followed through.

ANGRY BIRD

"I have a habit of un-learning."

My first son had said this following a heated debate on why he wasn't finishing what he started, why he wasn't following through on what he had agreed to do, and ultimately, why he was so much like his dad!

Again, good intentions are just cruel intentions if there is no follow-through. How many times have we made promises that we had every intention of keeping but just got distracted by an Angry Bird or a Tiny Wing or other creatures with the ability to fly and destroy? How often have others asked us for simple things, and we have just literally failed in the follow-through? Very little does more to undermine trust and relationship than unfulfilled promises.

THE JOY OF GUILT

I don't know about you, but this makes me feel kind of guilty or, to use a safer, more sanitized word, convicted. But maybe guilt is God's way of saying we can do more.

I realize there is a difference between guilt and conviction, but they feel the same, and do you know what? I'm personally thankful for that! It means I'm not dead inside or at least numb. Sure, there is "no condemnation in Christ" (Romans 8:1 NLT), but there's nothing like a bucket of ice-cold guilt to wake me up. And I'd rather have guilt than apathy.

And you now what else? I want to do more and collaborate more with God. I want to be awake and alert in the gardens of the living. I want to be trustworthy.

God does not love us because of what we do, but we want to do because we are loved.

True love is a giving love.

Twelve

Trust and Scars

A Life of Broken Restoration

ONE DAY

Today I will be masquerading as Thomas of the doubting kind. It's a far reach from the early, ill-advised 1980s costume I wore of "The Greatest American Hero," the blond, heavily permed-haired, reluctant superhero. And yes, full disclosure: I did perm my hair for that Halloween. It was method costuming. It was horrendous.

As with chapter 3 and Peter's life, I will now attempt to speak from Thomas's perspective, in the first person; Thomas aka Greg:

> When in doubt lock the door. We had journeyed with Jesus for years and had experienced so much. But now, our friend and Rabbi is dead.
>
> The other ten have locked themselves in, and they are still hiding. The threats are real, and I know I may be in danger, but it gets so claustrophobic in that room, just sitting around waiting. I get so tired of the waiting. We'd talked about

the good times and the relentless walking, but I just want to be real about it. Is Jesus coming back? Is what we he said true? I know he spoke of having faith, but all I'm questioning right now is if what he said and did can be trusted beyond death? Did Jesus fail? And if I'm really being honest, I'm wondering if it's me who has failed? Was there more we could've done to stop the madness of this execution? So I went for a walk to clear my head—this is what the Rabbi had taught us.

On my return, something had changed; everyone's posture was poised as if about to leap; it's then that I realized I had missed Jesus' supposed return to the house. John went on to tell me all about it, and I reckon he'll write about it as well. I know I'll be remembered as the outcast, something I've gotten used to but also something I kind of like, as it gives me an excuse to wander and to ask questions that others might consider immature or inappropriate.

John said Jesus just arrived literally out of nowhere, walked straight through the walls. Why didn't he knock? It says a lot without saying anything, as he knew he was always welcome, like friends who tell you not to knock but to just come in and help yourself to food.

To the hiding Disciples, he had said, "Peace be with you." I wish I could have heard that in his mixed-up accent. Peace has been ransomed by my doubt. But it's just like Jesus to walk through walls to bring peace. I can't remember the last time I walked through anything to bring peace or even love. I know I'm getting ahead of myself, but right now, having returned, I find myself sitting here just waiting, again, hoping Jesus will reappear; and all I'm building are walls of jealousy, insecurity, and unforgiveness. Why didn't they send someone for me?

John had told me that they had just stood there staring as the wall became flesh and spirit, a few of them dropped to their knees, a couple just slowly bowed as Jesus spoke of his Father sending him and in turn that he, our Rabbi, was going to send us. Don't get me wrong, they were happy to see Jesus, but joy is sometimes hard to describe and even harder to show.

Jesus had shown them his hands and side, the scars proof before them of the healing, of his actual death and now resurrection. Jesus had spoken candidly of his death as something that was necessary for our forevers; he's the only one I've ever met who seemed to actually chase death and seek out scars. But they kept their distance, laughing at me when I asked if they touched the scars, felt the raggedness of the healing? If my young nephews were here, they would ask me, "Is this appropriate?" As they knew, as well as I, that getting to these scars would mean stripping off so many layers. But Jesus isn't shy; remember when we were swimming or fishing or that day when he washed our feet.

But then . . . then he breathed on them. The Holy Spirit, the breath of heaven on the lips of Jesus now breathed into them, a warmth of air mixed with unexplainable fullness. They couldn't describe how this really felt, but the silence in the room and the tears in their eyes said it all. This was a comforter who would never leave us, even though Jesus might.

Where is he? It has been days. I'm getting bored and fed up with the waiting, but I dare not go for another walk.

Jesus had then given them an incredible power, the power of forgiveness, one that would annihilate sins; we didn't have degrees or collars or status; it wasn't necessary. I wonder what we will do with this awesome privilege? Hoard it, let it collect dust, or be as generous as the noonday sun? I just hope we don't try to control it; that could only lead to disaster, like withholding forgiveness in order to make myself feel better, more powerful, or give me ammo to tear someone else down. And what would I do with someone else's junk anyway? It's no good to me.

Why hadn't he just stayed here? Then I would've missed nothing. Last Friday will be a Friday I will never forget, but missing out on the Sunday return is tearing me up inside. I had missed the most cataclysmic moment of our time, the return of Jesus and the receiving of the Holy Spirit with my friends, my brothers, my family.

My absence was turning in to an abscess filled with doubt. I'd lash out at the others, shouting or mumbling or both; "Unless he stands right here in front of me and I touch his scars on his hands, his feet, and his side then I'm not going to believe anything, let alone that he's alive!" It was clear that my faith was being eroded by the lack of trust I had.

I was trying to be honest, but my vulnerability probably looked like arrogance.

For a whole week I sat there, not daring to move—just in case. I just sat there in the midst of their stories and celebrations, the can-you-believe-what-just-happened as well as the awkward silences as they'd realize they were "talking about it again" when I was sitting right there. Even as a child I'd always hated missing out.[1]

THE SUN

There once was a girl named Margot, who lived on rainy Venus. Venus only received sunshine for two hours every seven years. Margot, who had moved from Earth, would often tell her classmates of the sun. Her classmates were too young to remember the sun and so didn't believe her and resented her stories. All that can be done with the annoyance of desire, sometimes, is to lock away the reminder of what we don't have—though we may wish for it. So the other students grabbed the young girl and locked her in a closet. But to the shock and awe of the fellow students, on this day the sun did shine. They ran outside and played like they had never done before. But they had forgotten the girl who had always believed it could shine, and she had missed out on the glow and warmth of the sun on her skin.[2]

SCAB

There is that moment when the scab has coagulated, the blood congealed, and then you bend your knee or elbow undoing all the good of the healing, and you hear the sound and feel the breaking of the skin. You feel the sharp sting, and the warm liquids move to quickly plug the breach. I remember sitting for hours on end digging into the scab on my knee or my knuckle wondering if this would be a mark to boast of or the next story that I could tell of unimagined valor of a life lived with adventure and risk.

As a child, scars were a badge of honor, a bragging point, and a roll-up-the-trouser-leg-to-reveal moment in conversation. We would sit around for hours talking about the circumstances that brought this small white mark on our bodies.

What has happened to our fascination with scars, the desire to expose them at "show and tell"? These days we wear makeup to cover where the stone struck our forehead and long trousers to cover up the mark of courage that got us to the top branch of the tree.

The pursuit of scars, the pursuit of being human, has been replaced by the aimless groping for perfection, a perfection that will only be found when we stop looking for perfection in the created and begin finding Christ in our many, beautiful imperfections. Not in polished words of avoidance but in the author of creation.

So, do we seek scars? Do we look to experience emotional pain or spiritual chaos; of course we don't, but scars have a way of finding us. We are scar magnets; emotional, mental, and spiritual scars; just ask my three ex-girlfriends, my three stepmoms, or the pastor, the priest, and my belief.

Should we fear scars? Should we embrace them?

EIGHT DAYS

Thomas aka Greg:

> Eight days is long time. But in hindsight, it's only a blink when what you've hoped for walks through a wall.

> So I waited.

> Eight days full of anticipation, fear, hope, and doubt;
> Eight days of being the odd man out;
> Eight days of being the one who had missed the party.

> And then Jesus comes through the wall, just like the others had said, and he was there, right there, standing before me—I could hardly breathe.

> I shot a quick glance to the door and realized we had kept it locked. Why was it locked? Jesus had already come once and proved his coming again after the grave, yet we were still locking the door? It was only a moment, but it came very clear to me that we as followers of Christ

cannot lock away our lives, just waiting for another return. We obviously can't lock Jesus away, so why lock ourselves and the way we believe away? Now I'm annoyed with myself and still can't breathe. I reckon Jesus would've found me even if I hadn't sat here for eight days. He seems to be in the finding business.

Jesus stood there, a smile on his face—not of arrogance but of vulnerability. And I heard those three words that I was lacking in my depths, "Peace to you." Jesus is always leading with peace; I need to lead with peace more.

He looked right at me, right into me. He knew I had been missing before, and he came back, always coming back.

Then my living friend spoke, "Take your finger and examine my hands. Take your hand and stick it in my side."

I was shaking as my doubt began to fall off like dead skin, the exposed new skin more alive than ever. He unwrapped himself and, standing there exposed, he reached out his hands, then turning, showing his side, and revealing his feet. He must trust me—can I trust him?

Jesus was happy to enter my doubt, going as far as being raw and vulnerable—a vulnerable God before me, this doubter. He knew of my specific doubts and my need for specific actions, and he met me where I was, not where I should've been.

These healed wounds before me, how much these must have hurt, how much pain had he gone through for me? But why had he kept these scars? I could see and touch him, and I now knew he was alive, yet he kept these revealing scars. Of all the people who could've erased them, but here they were before me.

Was Jesus the imperfect perfect? These scars were a tangible proof that scars are not an imperfection but part of our stories to reveal.

He continued to speak as he always had during those long walks; the difference was that I was really listening now. "Don't be unbelieving. Believe." He wanted me to know him, again, in this new place of revelation.

My friend was so patient with me in the midst of my unbelief and doubt and confusion. This must be what beauty feels like.

I had recognized Jesus from the very first moment, but I couldn't bring myself to believe the impossible was possible—yet here was Jesus; the possible had been staring unrecognized in my face for far too long—even before it had entered the room.

Jesus then called me to a higher trust saying, "So, you believe because you've seen with your own eyes. Even better blessings are in store for those who believe without seeing."

An undeniable, indefinable shadow passed over

us at that moment, a foreshadowing of our near existence; a time when Jesus would only be present in Spirit, yet as close as a breath exhaled.

Jesus had considered my boldness as beautiful, my doubt even desired when pursuant of truth. And he never flinched when it came to vulnerability from that dark night in the garden to the brutality of the cross to his sacred scars.

My trust now fully restored, I determined myself to now get out of this locked room and begin to restore the severed trust that my friends and family had shared with me. I find it easier trusting the broken, for I am broken.

I now know that faith is not an ethereal mist or unattainable trick but that faith is a trust worked out in the physical, emotional, and spiritual.

When I doubted, Jesus told me to touch his scars; now when others doubt, I'm going to let them touch mine.[3]

TATTOO

Since leaving my childhood, my scars have become less obvious and yet somehow more pronounced. Hidden yet much more revealing; personally known secrets. What I used to wear proudly has become more covert. We are all messed up—welcome. But we are all redeemed. We all must fall before we can rise, for only one could rise without a fall.

Scars are a hideous wonder, the tattoo of the fallen. Yet to pursue scars is a misnomer; we don't want pain, we don't want to be bullied, we don't want death in our families, but scars, they pursue us. We need to stop and allow the breaking, welcome the healing, and permit the scars to form. For a scar speaks of healing itself, of a time gone through, of redemption found—We are all a "cold and broken hallelujah."[4]

We need to somehow embrace the flaws that define us, allow others to see the redeemed in this existing mess. I should offer my fears, flaws, anger, disappointment, confusion, the way I fail, the ways I flail, the way I hurt as a way to get back to who we truly are—pure and broken, damaged yet redeemed goods.

If we look long enough, we can see our own reflections in the scars of the "others." We are the same.

Share your stories, your scars, and begin to trust again.

Our scars are our common story.

Yet these days we spend more time highlighting the differences, that which is uncommon.

Do you want to learn again to trust one another? Speak and listen the others' stories. Show your scars. Your scars tell our story. This is where trust incubates. We might not like them—whether it's personal or institutional—but our scars define and refine us.

If we seek the common in our scars, in our stories, we will find the change. And I want change. Enough of all this distrust. I want to trust again.

Scars, our humanity, our stories, are the hard currency of our commonality. Trust is the bones under the skin of our living.

We are the seekers of the common and finders of the change.

SCARS = SCARS

Life is not about survival but about living it, wounds and all. We just need to stop pretending because scars = scars. Jesus maintained these wounds, the perfect retaining imperfections, amplified tattoos of the One broken.

Sometimes I think it would be easier to just ignore that which hurts, that which makes me feel, that which has a way of defining me and that which in time allows me to love others from the depths of my soul and not from my skin's surface. But scars remind us *how* we've lived and *what* we've lived *from*, as well as *what* we love *for*. And it is in that place that we find hope from God for others and for ourselves.

Being human is living with your insides out; created pure, but tainted and brought back. Being human is living with our flaws on the outside so that others may not fear to trust God. Our scars are a bridge of trust to Jesus, just as his were to Thomas.

Being human is about the amplification of the Creator and about becoming who we truly are—scars and all.

And I pray, Wounded Healer, show me how to heal and forgive from my own wounds, and may we be compassionate when others doubt, just as you are when I doubt.[5]

When we doubt, Jesus tells us to touch his scars; when others doubt, we need to allow them to touch ours.

Scars are our common stories. Trust is our common future.

Thirteen

Trust and Honor

The Radical Solidarity of Service

"The sole meaning of life is to serve humanity."
—Leo Tolstoy

DISCOVER BEAUTY

Whiskey and cardboard are hardly the best insulation, but when you're sleeping rough on the rain-drenched streets of London, they can quicken the sun's arrival.

They are wanderers. She is an artist. She quickly found they had more in common than met the original eye; an artist sees, as do wanderers.

She approached the four huddled men and slowly built trust by not crossing the street when passing them in the early morning, by leaving a sugar-laden tea for them to wake to, by getting to know their names. Between these weatherworn people and the artist grew a mutual trust, the artist eventually inviting them to spend time with her in the warmth of her studio. The artist painted their images, the grooves of the dense oil matching the grooves of the weatherworn men exquisitely. It wasn't long before curiosity lifted the communal brush and they all began painting on their own canvases. The men began painting the kind artist's image.

The artist's show was exhibited in central London. Her paintings arranged and priced. But four additional paintings hung alongside the artist's, the paintings by the weatherworn men. Standing proudly but with shocked faces—their paintings were on sale for hundreds of pounds. As the night progressed, they began to realize that the artist's paintings were actually selling for thousands of pounds—even the ones of themselves. They approached the artist and inquired, "Why do your paintings cost so much more than ours?"

The artist, feeling slightly embarrassed, hoping that she hadn't offended these men, began to explain that she was an established artist and this show had been organized long before she had met them . . . they cut her off saying, "I think you're misunderstanding our question. Our paintings of you are only priced in the hundreds of pounds, yet your paintings of us are thousands; it's just that we never thought we were worth so much."

Trust cultivates honor. Honor reveals value.

If we want to restore trust, we must hunt for beauty, as beauty is found at the well of a trusted place.

HONOR

Honor seems to be one of those words that died out with World War II veterans, curtsying, and *Little House on the Prairie*.

Saint Paul writes, "Be devoted to one another in love. Honor one another above yourselves" (Romans 12:10 NIV).

Honor reveals and generates the restorative process of relationship. The disconnect between humanity and itself, and between humanity and God, doesn't stand a chance in the face of true honor. Honor is the greenhouse for pure trust.

But frustratingly, like every good thing we seem to get our hands on, honor gets broken and needs to be rediscovered or indeed created afresh.

The ingredients of honor are found in many places—some obvious, most not. They are awakened in many ways, some obvious, most not. Yet devotion and perseverance stand out as committed revealers of honor, and stories of this dynamic duo can be conduits to creating stories of our own.

A RELUCTANT CROWN

There were once two kings; both broken, one insane.

David wore a wobbly, hard-fought-for, unexpected crown—but a crown nonetheless; and though it took decades to sit upon his head, the crown was always upon his heart.

In the Books of 1 and 2 Samuel, David's life is a study in honor and dishonor. But true honor is more likely found in a street fight than a garden party, as honor amplifies as a grace under pressure. (A slight disclaimer, though I am a bit of weakling, I would far rather be in a street fight than a garden party—those little cakes terrify me!)

David's life has a way of encapsulating all that I love and

hate about humanity, all that I love and hate about myself. David's life had so much promise, so much to emulate; yet as a king, his life had so many broken promises and so much that makes me want to regurgitate. To emulate and to regurgitate are so close on life's spectrum. A polite way to refer to David's story is as a "cautionary tale." But if you were Uriah or Rizpah, it would read differently (see 2 Samuel 11:15; 21:10). Yet it would be lackadaisical of me to think this level of darkness and light is only found in Old Testament kings; it is also found in me. So as we reveal David's kaleidoscope of a life, let it also reveal us. (I'm just glad my deepest regrets are not written in the most printed book on the planet!)

Let's look at David's life as if it were a ticker tape scrolling on a 24/7 news channel along with Pixar stocks, celebrity breakups, and overthrown governments.

As a boy, David is called out of his family as the anointed one and becomes a local folk hero; he kills a lion, a bear, and a giant; and he can play music. David definitely had inherited or cultivated the x-factor, but with it came the ridicule of those who had yet to discover their own beauty.

David moves to the big city and gets a gig in the palace, carrying armor and fighting the suicide missions of King Saul. This Saul, who would never become a Paul, is a king rapidly sliding into insanity. As it is with insanity, paranoia makes a good partner in a tragic slow dance. When the threatened, mad King Saul requests David's presence, David runs there, and as anyone would do when called by a king, he gives his best; meeting the king's request, he sings.

The king, feeling his grasp on his own wobbly crown slipping in the midst of a this younger, more virile king-to-be does as any threatened, mad king would do: he throws spears. David says nothing but moves his feet fast enough to avoid the projectiles, and in that, honors God's chosen and anointed king.

I've never really understood the anointing-to-sanity ratio. If I were God (and we can all be thankful I am not) and handing out silk sashes with "anointed" written across them, then I would have some terms and conditions applying: "Warning: The amount of anointing directly correlates to the amount of love given; the less the love, the less anointing. Your anointing will evaporate as your love dilutes."

But David never throws a spear back. He never throws a spear back.

WISDOM WITH FACIAL HAIR

You can easily tell when someone has been hit by a spear. He turns a deep shade of bitter. David never got hit. Gradually, he learned a very well kept secret. He discovered three things that prevented him from ever being hit.

One, never learn anything about the fashionable, easily mastered art of spear throwing. Two, stay out of the company of all spear throwers. And three, keep your mouth tightly closed.

In this way, spears will never touch you, even when they pierce your heart.[1]

If I could reprint the whole book *The Tale of Three Kings* by the mustachioed Gene Edwards here, I would. It is rare to find a book that so consistently challenges me, those I love, those I have thrown spears at, and those who have thrown spears with such thorough precision at me. It digs the deeper infection out of the seeming flesh wounds and replaces it with lasting cures.

BURN THE MANUALS

How many times have I wanted to throw spears back—to get my own back—in my work, in my home? How many times have I actually thrown back or initiated the humiliating dishonor of a thrown spear?

How often have I sat for hours, even days, whittling the tip of a spear, the words that would, if said just right, pierce any heart. The roll of the spear in my hands feels almost natural, the grip of the wood suffocating perspective, the throw far too accurate; my posture proud and strong, hiding a trembling and weak man just afraid of looking inside.

But David never did. He let them rattle about and pile at his feet.

An unthrown spear is a person's honor bright.

A PATIENT CROWN

Dishonor was humiliated in the exposure of true honor. The mad king now sat high and exposed. Dishonor hides true intentions, but honor exposes true intentions.

The biggest test of my honor today was reaching the last shopping cart on a slow-walk footrace with an eighty-year-old man and his Zimmer Frame. And after a lifting and a shaking and a wrestling it free, having to contemplate whether to give the last trolley to the elderly gentleman or not—such a test of honor. If spears were being thrown at any point in the scenario, I would've happily retreated to the air-conditioned safety of my car and its talk radio.

At least David had a decent reason to run—and many of us do. But we also may have a better reason to stay.

The king in his madness orders death, and the hunt for David ensues. David flees to a cave. The mad king hunts him down. Unable to find David, the king pees—even kings urinate. (1 Samuel 24:3; this is more likely a result of too much liquid than a protest at the lack of finding David.)

Hand on sword, David sneaks up on the king and, instead of killing him, spares the cruel ruler's life; later David and his scout sneak to within a spear's length of the king.

> Abishai said, "This is the moment! God has put your enemy in your grasp. Let me nail him to the ground with his spear. One hit will do it, believe me; I won't need a second!" But David said to Abishai, "Don't you dare hurt him! Who could lay a hand on God's anointed and even think of getting away with it?" (1 Samuel 26:8-9 *The Message*)

Twice David could've brought down the madness of a kingdom of shame; twice he restrained himself from the carnage. David must have had a deep trust that if God was a God of justice then a day of reckoning was coming—but sometimes the sunrise takes the longest when you're waiting for the horizon to break.

You cannot rush into honor. Honor must marinate.

The hunt continued. Bodies piled up. The mad King Saul died. More bodies piled up.

Seven hard years in the palace of madness dancing at the tip of a spear, fifteen years on the run from madness in the shadow of a spear, and then honor manifests—David becomes king.

David served—for honor is given, not taken. And honor restores trust to a kingdom prone to insanity. King David ascended to the throne, without a spear thrown, through service, humility, and honor. David established trust in the midst of a hailstorm and the carnage of spears, in the midst of dishonor and distrust.

A BROKEN CROWN

Let's be completely transparent; we cannot dismiss the bloodthirsty element of David's life. King David's rule was not without its own descents into massive amounts of lust-filled and control-seeking dishonor through abuses of power, breeding distrust in those who loved him most. This is where I struggle most with the histories and his-trionics of the stories we tell. They smell of beauty and honor and at the same time reek of pride, dishonor, and death. David, after being stalked by the abuse of power, descended into that which he had so proficiently avoided. Pride and a newfound sense of entitlement were a self-imposed slide of razor blades, dropping him into not just the using of spears for others to dodge but for a king to kill with. He, having not thrown a spear while following, was stockpiling and throwing them while leading. I, too, have sadly been here as a leader and hope to never return.

Trust restorers need to burn the instructional manuals of spear creation.

The weeds of pride choke honor out. As we grow into leaders—and don't fool yourself, we are all leaders—we cannot forget the lessons that we learned when following, and for the love of God and all creation, we can no longer replicate the past while growing complacent in the ascent to a throne. Thrones are overrated. Tear down your throne, dismantle the walls, and restore trust from a place of realized humility, from the ground beneath our feet.

There is constant temptation to ascend through dishonor and my own crafty means and to then remain ascended through the same divisive means. But the hard road of honor, of restoring trust, is found on the consistently hard road of service. Service keeps the ego of kings, queens, and kingdoms in check.

Trust restorers burn their own thrones. Humble service is a proficient incendiary.

WOMEN OF THE WELL

The concrete machine gun turrets, still warm from decades of a dictator's oppression, now housed sheep. It was the early 1990s, and I would have ten days to spend in the mountains of Albania, a decried atheistic nation, only a couple of years after the fall of communism. Fear, ever present as a spear, was palatable, and sadness could be sensed in the new, yet to be found, freedom of open markets and bootleg cigarettes.

I had joined a small group of zealous missionaries and

together we took a forty-hour train and boat journey to a remote village, which was a four-hour donkey ride from the mountain village. Isolated, with little food, no money, and zero language, we were definitely in over our heads.

On our arrival, the family of six we were staying with greeted us with open arms. To make room for us, they had moved out into the animal stable. I whispered a short prayer and admonished myself, hoping this wouldn't be the only thing we would do for this village—make them homeless.

Looking around, one thing that became quite obvious was that we were in need of water. I, being young (then) and full of energy (then), found two buckets and wandered to the watering hole that provided the only fresh water for miles. After walking the very steep, narrow, and winding mile-long path, I arrived to see a queue of thirty Albanian women waiting for their moment to fill their containers; an arduous task in that there was only slightly better than a drip coming from the rock.

The look of shock on the faces of the women said it all, "A man fetching water!" They insisted on filling and carrying my bucket; I refused. They insisted on letting me jump the queue; I was forced.

But when I got to the top of the queue, I just looked back in amazement that they, in this heat, wanted to serve me, an imperfect stranger.

Then I had one of *those moments*, one you'd like to reproduce daily but one that only comes along once in a while, like a falling star (or maybe I just need to look more often):

175

it was to be a simple epiphany. Maybe simplicity is the defining factor of epiphanies, life found in the extraordinarily ordinary. I turned around and one by one filled their buckets, pots, pans, and chipped porcelain teapots. Over the next ten days, I would find myself spending literally ten hours a day at the front of that queue, filling and carrying water buckets and laughing without the language. I was accepted, a vast stranger with no cultural understanding or words to express who I was.

On the final day, I dragged our translator with me down to the watering hole to say good-bye; it was the first time I'd been accompanied there. All the women gathered around asking, "What is wrong with this boy that makes him so different?"

The answer was so simple that I feel embarrassed to even write it here. (Then again, sometimes I feel like I've overcomplicated what my faith should be about.) I said, "Jesus is what is wrong with me." They laughed loudly and asked, "Who's Jesus?"

We spent the next forty minutes chatting about my life in America, theirs under Communism and its atheistic government, and how faith was one thing they were never allowed to speak of.

That day, I learned a lot about those beautiful women and about myself.

That day, I was found by the women of the well.

When service reveals honor and restores trust, words are not necessary.

Service is inseparable from honor.

Without sacrifice of self, there is no honor.

RADICAL SOLIDARITY

It took me far too long to realize, and it has become far too easy for me to forget, that service is a radical solidarity: an honor-inducing, trust-restoring elixir. It is in serving that God is realized and we find ourselves, as God is most easily found in the service of others.

Young David understood this, the artist got this, the women at the well understood; service is honor.

Jesus got this: incarnation is the ultimate restorative element of trust. The Creator's incarnation is the personification of honoring creation.

In my life and as you'll have read in this book, Philippians 2 is pretty much my soul tattoo.

These verses speak of honor, of service, of equality, and of an incarnational restoration of trust:

> If you've gotten anything at all out of following Christ, if his love has made any difference in your life, if being in a community of the Spirit means anything to you, if you have a heart, if you care—then do me a favor: Agree with each other, love each other, be deep-spirited friends. Don't push your way to the front; don't sweet-talk your way to the top. Put yourself aside, and help others get ahead. Don't be obsessed with getting your own advantage. Forget yourselves long enough to lend a helping hand.
> Think of yourselves the way Christ Jesus thought

of himself. He had equal status with God but didn't think so much of himself that he had to cling to the advantages of that status no matter what. Not at all. When the time came, he set aside the privileges of deity and took on the status of a slave, became human! Having become human, he stayed human. It was an incredibly humbling process. He didn't claim special privileges. Instead, he lived a selfless, obedient life and then died a selfless, obedient death—and the worst kind of death at that—a crucifixion.

Because of that obedience, God lifted him high and honored him far beyond anyone or anything, ever." (Philippians 2:1-11 *The Message*)

Ever.

Honor is intentional living.
Honor leverages what we have for others.
Honor restores trust.
Honor reveals honor.
When we honor one another, we reveal him who is honor.
Honor is our radical solidarity.

Fourteen

Trust and Home

The Sound of Crashing Tables in Sacred Spaces

THE BLUE GLOVES ON SEACOURT STREET

"For twenty-four hours, use these anytime you enter into this room."

Blue nitrile gloves. I've seen these disposable exam gloves before in crime scenes in movies and on TV—they are as familiar as coffee shops and iPads. But I'd never had them handed to me by a police officer, in my own bedroom with the sentence, "For twenty four hours, use these anytime you enter into this room."

We arrived home on that Saturday night, and I knew something wasn't right. You know that feeling, like something is missing, like the moment you look down and your mobile phone or jacket or first-born has gone walkies. That feeling twists and turns over in your most inner guts, the warning lights flash and your senses are heightened, every hair on your skin electric and aware.

There is someone in my home. My home. My family's home. Our sanctuary of safety.

When you see three distinct, unwelcome shadows, the grizzly bear inside you emerges, rises up, and roars. You feel protective, you feel vulnerable, yet you still advance, terrified. Standing and roaring, "Get out of my home!"

Three very long seconds lapse in the increasingly small room as they face you—one with a crowbar—and then just as quickly they turn, tripping over one another in order to get out of the small window now off its hinges. You continue to run toward the fear, shouting, "Get out of my home! Get out of my home!"

Home is a place created by life being lived with one another. Home is a place that, together, we have nurtured and wrestled to get to a place where vulnerabilities are safe to roam. To have this rattled is to throw everything off balance. To have this disturbed is to want to fight for it to return.

My wife, on that night, feeling a similar but more acute surge of fear and protectiveness, is running around to get the license plate number—we want to catch them, we want names, revenge, a conviction, we want justice; but it will never come. They spat in her face as they drove away.

My kids didn't sleep that night. Neither did my wife and I. My younger boy had nightmares of being taken away. My older boy didn't want to return home. My daughter cried when we did.

On my daughter's Facebook page the next morning she wrote:

"i was terrified that sum1 was in my house. i thought where i live was the safest place ever . . . i had the worst sleep of my life last nite . . . . i woke up early this morning and i wish it never happened."

Our peace wasn't just disrupted; it was totally shattered, seemingly obliterated. This is our home; a place to be ourselves, to laugh, to feel secure, to walk about uninhibited by fear, to be naked. Now we wanted locks and alarms and protective armor.

Could we see a way past this? Could we find a way through the fear? Could we trust the sanctity of these four walls? Could we find peace in our home again?

Maybe our peace was only interrupted.

HOUSE VS. HOME

This experience—while unwelcome—had me looking at my home differently and approaching my home with a fear and trepidation that had me asking, *When have I ravaged the feeling of home from my own house, from others' houses? When have I used my home wrongly? As a place of control and personal gain?*

I slowly realized that, when I do, I am like the robber who broke into our home. (We are all the home we all share.)

The parallels and distinctions between house and home are limitless for those of us in God's house these days. I say house, as I feel, at large, it is no longer a home, a place of peace, security, vulnerability, authenticity. The house of God has been burgled by its residents, and the traces of home only just linger in the recesses and crevasses of a time past. We are in a time of innocence lost as we have tarnished innocence many times and will continue to do so. I am a resident who has robbed himself of a church, a home of God. But there has been a far more subtle grand theft, an eroding heist by those who seek to control God, the Great Uncontrollable, God who is free beyond freedom.

I've grown up going to the Houses of God, but whatever happened to the homes of our Father?

Church is a place created by life being lived among ourselves. Church is a place that, together, we have nurtured and wrestled with to get to a space where vulnerabilities are safe to roam. To have this rattled is it to throw everything off balance. To have this disturbed is to want to fight for it to return.

The broken experiences of church that I have lived through—while unwelcome—had me looking at church differently and approaching church with a fear and trepidation that had me asking, *When have I used God's house wrongly? For my own gain? How have I ravaged the feeling of home from other's homes, from God's?*

We are the robber who broke into house of God. We are all the church home we share.

How do we begin to wrestle the bride back from the crime scene that is the church of today? The veil covered in the chalk dust. I know this is coming across very judgmentally, and the assumption would be, could be, that this author is one bitter, wounded, messed up, and angry man—yes, this is all true—but I want our Father's home back. I want it restored. As you'll have read, I have seen churches split, communities break down, and the body of Christ crumble—I've walked on that broken glass and have thrown stones at its very stain. My wrestle is with the church that no longer feels like a home. And when a house is not a home, of course, we leave. Why would we stay? The result? We have become the emigration generation, with the largest exodus from church-based spirituality in any time in history. They have been crowded out by unmet expectations, prejudices, and broken promises.

OLIVER STREET AND SUQ EL QATANIN STREET 1.0

The disciples of Jesus must have been seriously fit, catlike, to be able to get up and go within a second's notice. It's no wonder Jesus told them just to take what they could carry. I know this was for many spiritual reasons, but it was also very practical. Whenever Jesus got word of something needing to happen, from the death of a relative to the stones being gathered around a vulnerable woman, Jesus would just go without hesitation. These days it seems like we need to design a logo and run a fund-raiser just to pursue justice. But injustice is not so patient. And justice is not copyright controlled.

I'm sure Jesus and his disciples already knew about the stuff being sold in the temple, but then, just then, at that very moment, Jesus was fed up and action was needed (see Matthew 21:12-14). True, he took the time to make the whip—the phrase never take a knife to a gunfight comes to mind—and with passion expounding in his veins, he made his way down to the temple. I picture the look on his face to be like my mom's when one of the neighbor boys had taken my bike, giving me a skinned knee at the time. A strong determination in my mother had led the way. Justice at five feet zero inches was walking down my hometown sidewalk of Oliver Street to get back what had been taken.

Only height was in the difference as Jesus pushed through the crowds near the temple on what is now called Suq El Qatanin Street.

Matthew was in fast pursuit of a Rabbi looking to take back what had been taken. Like an embedded reporter he observed in close proximity passion personified.

> Jesus went straight to the Temple and threw out everyone who had set up shop, buying and selling. He kicked over the tables of loan sharks and the stalls of dove merchants. He quoted this text: My house was designated a house of prayer; You have made it a hangout for thieves. (Matthew 21:12-14 *The Message*)

John, standing at Matthew's side, both possibly out of breath yet exhilarated by the moment of a purifying chaos, was likely to be frantically trying to commit this moment to memory while Jesus was shouting, "Get your things out of here! Stop turning my Father's house into a shopping mall!" That's when his disciples remembered the Scripture, "Zeal for your house consumes me" (John 2:16-17 *The Message*).

I can see the gaggle of disciples circling the inner courts, close to Jesus but not too close, questioning yet protecting, eager yet hesitant, but with hearts on fire as the inner of the courts began to breathe again—the excess of consumption having been removed from its chest. Suffocation relenting to a redemptive resuscitation. Matthew then observes the aftermath of the crime scene, "Now there was room for the blind and crippled to get in. They came to Jesus and he healed them" (Matthew 21:14 *The Message*).

Now there was room for those most in need.

Jesus was returning the temple to its original reason for being—keeping the sacred places sacred—as a place of worship for everyone.

Freedom is the sound of crashing tables in sacred spaces.

Trust was restored through the turning over of tables.

FISH-N-CHIPS ON CHURCH STREET

Years ago I met a refreshing priest. He was kind and knowledgeable, a risk-taker placed in a country parish. The joke used to be that if you were driving through these parish towns and blinked, you'd miss them. Unfortunately, the desire to get somewhere without experiencing the journey has all but wiped away the knowledge of these one-pub, one-shop, one-church towns; the seemingly wonderful criteria of an Irish town, including the one I live in—though we now have two churches!

The location of the church in which this refreshing priest served was, in terms of accessibility to his parishioners, perfect. Maybe a little too perfect—right in the center of this intimate town. The church was changing, and the status quo was becoming uncomfortable. The older generations of stalwarts were dying out, and as urbanity sprawled, the younger families were moving in. With these younger families came the fear and the future and possibly the biggest fear of the church: teenagers. On the weekends, these teenagers who had nothing else to do would meet to drink in the church's cemetery before hitting the fish-n-chips shops for a deep-fried, battered sausage and bag of chips. When it rained, they had to run for shelter, lately taken to congregating under the arches of the church, not "their" church but just a conveniently located, architectural umbrella.

The priest noticed this and had to take action. But no, he didn't chase them off brandishing a pitchfork, and no, he didn't call the police. What he did was far riskier. He engaged. He would leave the comfortable fireside at his rectory and go outside, risking embarrassment to be present with the teenagers. Seeing them wet and in need of a place to sit, he would open the front of his church and welcome them in where they could sit on the prostrated graves of the founders of the church. What better place to sit than on a structure made for rest? Sure these teenagers were rough around the edges, and sure it took time for them to settle into their new surroundings, but within the month they were chatting away at volume, staying later than they should have been welcome and yet still throwing their rubbish into the corners of the old church. But they were also wondering. Wondering who this priest was. Wondering why he opened up the building with no judgment. And wondering why he would come in and clean up after them as they left, without saying a word. They wondered so much that they started turning up on Sunday mornings to hear the old priest speak. Trust being restored through the silent collection of greased fish-n-chips papers.

Not wanting it to end there, the old priest approached his vestry and inquired if they could do more, perhaps using some money that had been left recently by a parishioner who had died. He suggested that they open the front gates of the churchyard farther, install lighting, and even extend the arches to allow more teenagers to enter, to find covering. At the same meeting, another suggestion came forward. The town was expanding. They all knew this because of the volume of traffic they sat in daily and the growing queues in the grocery store. Housing estates were going up everywhere, and one estate in particular was almost touching the border of the churchyard just over the three-foot stone wall. They knew that this meant access between the estate and the church grounds, and so they knew this meant trouble. The suggestion was put forward to build the wall higher to keep the debris and the "wild ones" out. The priest was puzzled at the contradictory suggestions but determined as he pleaded his case to the other six vestry members. A show of hands was taken. Six-to-one. The walls would be built higher. The gates would remain locked and inaccessible.

PIRATE'S TREASURE

Why do we fear those who are most in need? Why do we fear granting access to that which has given us access? God didn't say "Welcome" with one breath and "Quick, go run and hide" with another. Yet, I confess, sometimes going to church feels just like sin. It feels kind of good during it, but afterward you're just left confused. Is this admission a denial of God? No.

Are we afraid that others might see that we once had a need and still do? Do we fear that others around us might see the cracks in the visage even after we boast of redemption? The doubts we have of an Almighty, though we rant of our personal knowledge of him? The confusion of unanswered prayers in the midst of everything being broken, the lack of peace in the noise of guilt not yet removed by the Jesus that we hold high as the Savior? Are we afraid that they will see our frustration with and lack of insight in the Bible that we have lauded as the answer to every problem? Are we afraid that they will see our deepest desire to stop pretending? Do we fear that they will be drawn to God just to be disappointed at the pace of redemption? Do we fear they are just like us?

We cannot control grace; we do not possess the ability to limit God's love, yet that is what we constantly do. We sit behind our high walls or high ideals or high concepts pontificating and limiting access to that which is actually free and available to all. We hold our mini-kingdoms just out of reach—just like someone teasing a child with sweets. Understandably, that child will soon tire of our taunts and search for satisfaction elsewhere. What kind of father gives a snake when an egg is asked for, a razor blade for a toy, sand for water?[1]

If we are to be trusted again as the church, as people who want to gather in the name of God, we need to eradicate the parish boundaries, the walls that surround our identities. We can no longer be concerned with our name on the door and the boast over coffee of the largest under-sixties population. It can no longer be about the household that we grew up in or the building that we were dragged in to. Entitlement is a pirate's treasure.

Together, we need to look over our fences at those who surround us with the same deep needs that burn in our veins. We need to see those without hope find hope, those who carry guilt find freedom, and those without homes know home. You do not need to be pure to enter through these doors because this church is a sick ward, an insane asylum, an intensive care unit, and a garden. We need to remove the acts of access that confound grace. There are no acts that bring redemption. There is only grace. There is only Jesus. Church should be the Wild West community of our culture today, the no-holds-barred reality in today's society. Church should be a place that does not suppress hunger but rather creates it. Church should be a place where an incarnational trust comforts and cures the discarnational distrust that litters our entrances, both in buildings and bodies. A place that does not hide its limited knowledge of grace but projects it. A place with no walls and only open gates. The church should be a wild deer in the urban centers. The mess should be on the apron of God. Justice is blind and equal—surely our grace should be that and much more.

Trust is restored through the tearing down of fences and the turning over of altars.

"So let's go outside, where Jesus is, where the action is—not trying to be privileged insiders, but taking our share in the abuse of Jesus. This 'insider world' is not our home" (Hebrews 13:13-15 *The Message*).

Jesus turned tables over in his Father's house, looking to lead a collective of table turners who will follow him throughout the generations, turning his house into homes.

OLIVER STREET AND SUQ EL QATANIN STREET 2.0

John, a disciple of Jesus, continues his investigative and participative confluence writing:

But the Jews were upset. They asked, "What creden-
tials can you present to justify this?" Jesus answered,
"Tear down this Temple and in three days I'll put it
back together."

They were indignant: "It took forty-six years to
build this Temple, and you're going to rebuild it in
three days?" But Jesus was talking about his body as
the Temple. Later, after he was raised from the dead,
his disciples remembered he had said this. They then
put two and two together and believed both what
was written in Scripture and what Jesus had said.
(John 2:18-19 *The Message*)

The architecture of the heart is always more complex than
bricks and mortar.

I want our homes back. I want our churches back. I want
our faith back. Sure, we'll most likely corrupt it all again,
but the time for passivity, apathy, and sleep are long past.
It is time to let a trust established rebuild.

ME STREET

Transformation can only begin in the soul, and that soul is
your own. It is and will always be easier to critique another
person, but it is the transformation of ourselves that is far
more difficult.

As Walter Brueggemann says, "The task of prophetic ministry is to hold together criticizing and energizing."[2]

This prophetic ministry, for me, includes ministry to the
church, with others, and of myself.

I love the critique of everything that isn't me, as it distances me from the danger of changing, and it helps me

procrastinate in my own transformation. But as the critique of my soul travels through the fear of my home on Seacourt Street, through the motherly justice of Oliver Street, down Suq El Qatanin Street, and past the church of high walls on Church Street, I must, if I am to ever see trust reestablished, continue this journey on Me Street.

"You realize, don't you, that you are the temple of God, and God himself is present in you? No one will get by with vandalizing God's temple, you can be sure of that. God's temple is sacred—and you, remember, are the temple" (1 Corinthians 3:16-17 *The Message*).

We are temples, God's homes; you know this, you've heard it shouted thousands of times from street corners and pulpits—my own voice hoarse from its proclamation.

We, too, are the desecrated houses of God; you know this, though we only speak of it in whispers and moans. Oh, how our body aches for home.

I'm curious: if it were possible to journey into our souls, what tables would we have carefully constructed? What are they cluttered with? Does it look like a shopping mall?

Have we kept the sacred places sacred?

What tables do we need to grab and turn over in our lives? Which ones do we need others to help with? What are the ones that only Jesus can turn over in our lives?

The unashamed love of Christ, which rushed to turn tables in the temple of Jerusalem and return it to its created purposes, also rushes to do the same for us today.

Pursue the turning of your own tables—making your body a home for God—and go and do the same *with* those around you. And trust will multiply quicker than shopping malls—and that's pretty quick.

The restoration of trust eradicates the infected distrust that clutters our lives, a purity restored through a love that turns tables over.

Ephesians 2:19-22 (*The Message*) says,

> That's plain enough, isn't it? You're no longer wandering exiles. This kingdom of faith is now your home country. You're no longer strangers or outsiders. You belong here, with as much right to the name Christian as anyone. God is building a home. He's using us all—irrespective of how we got here—in what he is building. He used the apostles and prophets for the foundation. Now he's using you, fitting you in brick by brick, stone by stone, with Christ Jesus as the cornerstone that holds all the parts together. We see it taking shape day after day—a holy temple built by God, all of us built into it, a temple in which God is quite at home.

A restored trust enables tables to be turned.

What is the sound of freedom? Freedom is the sound of crashing tables in our sacred spaces. Unforgiveness shattering on the floor; anger crashing to the ground; injustice being trampled underfoot; pride scattering; beauty found in the carnage of distrust.

From sacred churches to our sacred hearts, freedom is the sound of crashing tables in sacred spaces. Freedom is home, restored.

Find your table-turning passion. Follow it. Cultivate it.

Fifteen

Trust and Living

All Our Beautiful Castles

In solitude, our heart can slowly take off its many protec-
tive devices, and can grow so wide and deep that nothing
human is strange to it. . . . It is in this solitude that we dis-
cover that being is more important than having, and that
we are worth more than the result of our efforts.
                                    —Fr. Henri J. M. Nouwen[1]

REALITY

On Friday I watched a duck for five minutes.

With a dogged determination I wandered from the noise
of the traffic to the center of the park; though the hum
remains, the birdsong takes over.

Yet there is still noise; of future, of family, of where I trade
my eternal for the temporary, and my mind is weak at
allowing the internal traffic to overwhelm the peace that is
still approaching.

But as I sit quietly—past many heartbeats—the noise
subsides, the birdsong brings clarity, and I have stopped

struggling. I am now—if only for a glimpse—breathing in the deep.

The God we look for is the God that has already found us. Yet it is in places of silence and solitude where clarity is the loudest, where perseverance and perspective intertwine, where we lose our heavily cultivated false selves and stumble into and find our whole true selves. It can be as startling as catching a reflection of yourself after a long stay in a hospital and as freeing as deep, uncontrollable laughter.

In my life I have sought out places of solitude, as I'm rubbish at practicing solitude daily. And it was here in my solitude for five silent days—no eating, no speaking, no writing of this book—that I was approached by the guest master of Glenstall Abbey. He smiled, and I broke my silence.

Greg: "Well, now it's back to reality."

Br. Ambrose: "Don't let them take that away from you. This, too, is reality."

Just because it seems gentle doesn't means it's not radical. Reality is not found just in the busyness of day-to-day living but also in the glimpses of silence and solitude.

Silence and solitude allow the gentle and consistent tide of transformation. Silence—the subversive beauty that erodes the futility of the temporary.

It is these times when syllables and vowels and rhythms and notes of staccatoed definition begin to emerge and coagulate and speak to you without words. This is where you begin to know who and why you truly are.

WHO'S COMING WITH ME?

It's one of my favorite fish-filled exchanges in cinema, and it takes place in Cameron Crowe's movie *Jerry McGuire*. The main character, played by Tom Cruise, says, "I'm starting a new company, and the fish are coming with me. You can call me sentimental, but the fish are coming with me."

He continues, "Now, If you come with me, this will be the moment of something new, and fun, and inspiring in this GODFORSAKEN business. And we will do it together. So . . . Who's coming with me?"[2]

Jerry implores, "Who's coming with me? Who's coming with me?" Only one responds reluctantly. They exit the office building, fish and bowl in hand.

OK, I'm just gonna say it—don't judge me—but, for me, the Sermon on the Mount was Jesus' Jerry Maguire Speech. Jerry's speech formed in the silence and frustration of his hotel room. Jesus' speech formed in the silence and frustration of his mountaintop.

The Sermon on the Mount calls us into our humanity, recognizes reality, and says, "This is what needs to happen. Now, who's with me?"

CATTLE AND TREES

When we turn the corner while approaching the apex of the mountain, we find Jesus in the midst of a people who took their religion very seriously; their religion, arguably one of the most consistent, both good and bad influences on culture since day one. And Jesus is sitting there with a small group of fishermen and other blue-collar workers saying, "Are you with me?" He was reinventing that which surrounded them and recalibrating the missing parts; incarnational trust, hope, and love.

Following the intimate delivery of Jesus' raison d'être, the Sermon on the Mount, Saint Matthew wrote, "This was the best teaching they had ever heard" (Matthew 7:28 *The Message*). Many years later, both Billy Graham and Mahatma Gandhi agreed with him—Mr. Graham calling it the "greatest moral and social document the world has ever known."[3] Mr. Gandhi saying it "delighted me beyond measure."[4]

"Oh wait, I can top that," Jesus *never* said. But what an incredible start to an albeit short career in public discourse and revolution. Talk about pressure, though; your best talk right out of the blocks? I spent a good part of my teenage years speaking to cattle and trees just to practice speaking just in case I had the opportunity. Jesus nailed it right there and then—with no auto-cue—knowing that he was laying it down at the beginning: this is the life we need to live, and now I'm going to walk with you through it, saying, "These are words to build a life on" (Matthew 7:24 *The Message*). His Sermon on the Mount has even been called the first book of Jesus.

CULTURE OF A KING

After the teaching of the Sermon on the Mount, a speech that has its fingerprints on everything from the United Declaration of Human Rights to fridge magnets, this "self-portrait" of Jesus when lived out is the ultimate mandate for restorers of trust.

Again Matthew: "This was the best teaching they had ever heard."

But why? This could be answered thousands of ways, but here's my stab at it answering a small percentage of the "why." The Sermon on the Mount was and is a systematic disassembling of what was considered the kingdom of God at the time. Following the Sermon on the Mount, what was then, and what had been before, became just dim reflections.

Kingdoms of "gods" became the Thy Kingdom Come; the "cults of kings" became the Culture of a King; and a dismantling of a hypocritical false self became the living of a whole true life beyond perception. Not for self; it was instead to be fully for others.

Midway through the Sermon, Jesus sums it up in a few sentences: "In a word, what I'm saying is, Grow up. You're kingdom subjects. Now live like it. Live out your God-created identity. Live generously and graciously toward others, the way God lives toward you" (Matthew 5:48 *The Message*).

The Sermon on the Mount is the very bridge between distrust and trust, the road paved by the lyrical text of a humble king looking to reinstate trust.

LIVE

The full text of the Sermon on the Mount can be found in the Bible in Matthew 5–7. What I've done below in "130 words, 42 full stops, 1 Sermon on the Mount" is to distill, *in my humble opinion*, what could be considered, *by me,* the essence of Jesus' life mandate for us. (Were there enough disclaimers in that last sentence?)

May I suggest you take this to the silent places and allow yourself to marinate in the incredible life you've been called to live.

130 WORDS, 42 FULL STOPS, 1 SERMON ON THE MOUNT

Less of you, more of God.
Be lost, be embraced.
Be you, no more, no less.
Consume God. Be consumed by God.
Care.
Curate an inner life.
"Discover beauty in everyone." (Romans 12:17-21 *The Message*)
Discover beauty in everything.
Collaborate; celebrate others.
Don't fear.
Get in trouble for justice's sake.
Be present.
Flavor your world.
Shine on and on and on.
Don't compete, complete.
"Don't take yourself too seriously, take God seriously." (Micah 6:8 *The Message*)
Laugh more.
Honor selflessly.
Forgive flagrantly.
Cultivate unity.
Encourage.

Do not harm.
Be anti-death.
Love with abandon.
Stop pretending.
Lead with action not with words.
Follow through.
Be spontaneous in your generosity.
Serve without hesitation.
Crave simplicity.
Pursue silence.
Amplify grace.
Articulate your inner life.
Sing like no one is listening.
Worry no more.
Hope.
Restore trust.
Be. Do. Be.
Welcome all.

The Sermon on the Mount changes the way we see things, gives us perspective, flips our worldview from just hearing to going and doing: "These are words to build a life on."

The Sermon on the Mount is the blueprint for trust restoration. But my living is my amnesia. And I, Greg Fromholz, am a walking contradiction.

THE GREAT PRETENDER

Have you ever had the feeling that someone is following you? You know, that growing sense of dread and the fear that causes you to break out into a cold sweat and makes the hairs on the back of your neck stand on end? I found myself experiencing that sharp, eerie sensation a few years ago, as I took a shortcut through a dark Dublin alleyway. It was because coming up behind me was a homeless man, and I knew he was going to mug me. That's what those types of people do! Right?

His footfall was hurried and had an irritated, aggressive feel to it. I thought, *Oh great; this guy is going to jump me and take my no-money.* But then he spoke: "I'm not going to rob ya, I'm not going to hurt ya, I just have a question." I didn't believe him and was instead wondering, *Do I run now?* Against my better judgment, I stopped and listened skeptically (although I was keeping an eye out for an escape route). "Over there," he said, pointing to a group of seven people all in their later years, looking the worse for wear and clearly already very drunk at two o'clock in the afternoon. "That's my dad over there" he told me, "and he's fifty-three today."

The cynic in me quickly retreated, and the tension in my muscles relaxed, to be replaced by an uncomfortable sadness at the idea of a father and son living on the streets together. He continued speaking, humbly; "It's my father's birthday, we have no money, and it's been years since we've had a cake."

I had assumed the worst of this man from the start; I had been ready to turn away. In that moment I had failed. All he wanted was to celebrate his dad's birthday. He continued, "Please don't give us the money because we will spend it on drink. Could you buy us a cake?"

Guilt is sometimes a beautiful thing, the ugly but necessary stepsibling of conviction. That day the rhythm of guilt powered my legs straight to the nearest grocery store. I located the party aisle, and fueled by my guilt-buzz, I bought a cake, as well as party hats, streamers, a banner, matching napkins, and the candles you can't blow out.

I paid for the all the multicolored party gear and ran, chased by a thorough humbling, back to the alleyway. They invited me to stay for the party. That afternoon we sat there, party hats on, in that dirty alleyway singing "Happy Birthday," attempting to blow out candles, and eating cake. As I walked away from that group of men and women, I could hear them breaking into a "hip-hip-hooray!" for the fifty-three-year-old homeless man. But louder still was the ringing of failure in my ears.

Head held low, I walked away from there thinking: I've been someone following God for twenty years, this big God who loves me so much, and I knew all God wanted me to do was embrace them—but I'd become a professional Christian ignoring people, ignoring the forgotten, and pretending I have it all together.

I had been an undiagnosed hypocrite for the past few decades of my life, hiding it well beneath the veneer of "doing and having been done for me." Going to all the right church services, memorizing all the right verses, not dancin', not drinkin', not chewin', and always hopin'— silently—to go out with the girls who were. My lip-synch was fully sunk on the surface of it all, but I had a lot of company and an assumption of salvation.

I was living in a Christian green screen, a safe studio CGI with a steeple. Over the decades, I'd honed this skill, crafted the mirage, while becoming a professional Christian.

I didn't follow Christ so that I could just call out, "Hey, God loves you" from a sanitary distance and walk away, chucking in a coin for added feel-good, in place of human connection. I can't just reach out with the content to only feel the relief of the stretch, without its fulfillment. There is so much more. There is contact. There is the incarnate. There is life.

The homeless son of a homeless man shook me, the great pretender, from my failure and helped me see that my faith was about so much more than just existing. We've got to allow our faith to weave itself into our everyday fabric, beyond the catwalks of Sunday mornings and the perception of having it all together.

Until we've experienced real change in our lives, we can't expect to participate in the change in others. But it's hard to see when we ourselves are blinded. "It's hard to listen while we preach."[5]

We've got to move beyond perception and pseudo-reality and allow our faith to engage and become part of our everyday fabric, beyond the perception of having it all together and the constant auditions. Perception is a virus, and it accelerates decay.

From the Sermon on the Mount:

> Be especially careful when you are trying to be good so that you don't make a performance out of it. It might be good theatre, but the God who made you won't be applauding. . . . Knowing the correct password—saying "Master, Master," for instance—isn't going to get you anywhere with me. . . . All you did was use me to make yourselves important. You don't

impress me one bit. You're out of here. (Matthew 6:1;
7:21-23 *The Message*)

Gulp.

This is me; at times a more remote me, at times closer
than my very skin. Then the words of the Sermon on the
Mount return like a forgotten season, grasping my winter
to wring out the springtime.

No more excuses, no more pretending, no more profes-
sionals, for we are all amateurs of hope.

If we want trust to be restored to our relationships, then
we must be unafraid to show who we really are. Faith and
trust and relationships are all about finding one another
amid the mess of living. Faith and trust and relationships
are all about seeing the strings, allowing the paint to chip
and peel, the sand to be tracked in; the trip, the fall, and
the redemption in the midst of it all.

We need to get the notes wrong.
Sing out of key.
Stand in the aisles.
Shout in the silence.
Be silent in the noise.

The God who speaks is the God who says very little. The
God who can heal is also the God who sometimes doesn't
heal. The God of beauty is a God who allows the ugly, like
me in my hypocrisy-tattooed soul, to still follow him, to
even represent him.

We, the becoming, are those who step over that fear of
discovery, fear of being outed, fear of being exposed, fear

of being a fraud, a someone who doesn't have it all together, so that we can be truly whole. This confession will
go further to establishing trust than any amount of perfec-
tionist posturing.

The Sermon on the Mount shatters perceptions and kingdoms. The Sermon on the Mount leads us to the death
of professional Christendom. And today, my friends, is a
good day to die.

A life spent pursuing Jesus leads to a life reflecting and
refracting the Sermon on the Mount. A life spent pursuing
the Sermon on the Mount leads to Jesus and to a life lived
like Jesus.

ALL OUR BEAUTIFUL SANDCASTLES

I used to love building sandcastles. But trying to divert the
tide from washing them all away was always so futile. Yet
I would spend hours trying to hold back the tide. When
it finally crashed in, there was a feeling of sadness, exhil-
aration, inevitability, and relief; yet something new could
now be created and this time, hopefully, built with more
permanency.

The Sermon of the Mount refines like the tide, our temporary foundations becoming sand running through our
fingers.

This is why I attempt to live for others.
This is why I pray.
This is why I practice the spiritual disciplines.
This is why I go on retreats of silence.

Because it's in these places that I "allow" the eroding tide of Christ to rid me of my personal sandcastles and build solid foundations for living.

We can now begin to rebuild our faith and churches with trust and love.

COCOON

Society's rejection of the gospel being preached by churches today is due to a thankfully but painfully exposed hypocrisy; and hypocrisy is a tsunami to the elaborate sandcastles built in Jesus name.

We all build them and love to take the time doing so— even if we are aware of the impending tide—and we still try to stop the waves as they reach our trenches dug to save our castles. But the tide will always come, and the waves of spiritual maturity will break us down—I call this horrible at times and grace at others.

This is not an enjoyable process—refinement—yet it's inescapable. Becoming spiritually fit is the process of eroding all that is false. With this tide comes a knowledge of peace and joy deep down in the midst of all the storms. Did I enjoy having my wobbly faith reflected to me by the birthday party in the alleyway? No, as it was a large wave to all my beautiful castles. Yet I want that holy dissatisfaction, a grating irritant that drives me to the depths of living.

Our lives are lives worth persevering, worth preserving. "Suffering produces perseverance; perseverance, character; and character, hope" (Romans 5:3-5 NIV). This is more easily read than lived. The tide is a persistent refining of our character, revealing hope, trust, and love. There is a mutual perseverance between God and humanity; one without need constantly revealing, the latter full of need looking and finding.

What sandcastles have you built, what barriers to the tides of refinement?

Do you want to find peace? Do you want to find trust, again? Do you want to find yourself? It's here buried beneath all of our beautiful castles—consumption, assumption, disillusionment and disappointment. Together we need to disassemble and dig through the destruction, the rubble, the congealed sand. It happens as we persevere to the silent depths with God.

I don't want to exist in a weak-walled cocoon.
I want to be free and secure in him who is unaffected by
    the seasons and their storms.
I want my castles to crumble so that I may live strong for
    God and others.

BLUEPRINT

The Sermon on the Mount didn't just erode castles. It turned tables, altars, churches, nations, and hearts.

The Sermon of the Mount is found in soul-eroding storms, in wide-open spaces. It is a new language, a blueprint, a soul-print for living.

The Sermon on the Mount is the periodical chart for restoration using the elements that make us who we are, combining to make such beauty.

Together let us take deep breaths and dive the depths. Let us welcome the large waves, and let us embrace the tide.

Sixteen

Trust and Collaboration

Seek the Common

FIND THE CHANGE

Absolutely everything in the total history of everything has come about through collaboration. This universe is a collaboration machine. Your body is a collaborating miracle.

Change will never come without collaboration.

FOUR STOOLS

The courage was as palpable as the ketchup and saliva smeared across the faces of the brave young men and women who had chosen to collaborate toward a new future. A collaboration that would cost lives and reveal a hatred that is still an open wound in America and beyond. Prejudice masquerades as many an angel. Yet many an angel gives a life for justice.

It's February 1960, and the weather is still crisp. Winter is refusing to lose its grip, but the springtime is just around the corner, and winter cannot hold it back.

The Greensboro Four, young men determined to thaw the long winter of segregation, are heading for a cup of coffee. They walk through the door, past the wood-sided, color televisions, past the fine bone china teacups, and past the suspicious stares of the Woolworth's employees. Determination has a scent, justice a beautiful fragrance. 132 South Elm Street in Greensboro, North Carolina, would never be the same. Neither would America.

The young students walked past the counter where they were "allowed" to be. It is the days of segregation, and everything from lives to hospitals to toilets to coffee counters were color-coded. The eyes of those four young African American men were locked on the counter that had a sign reading "Whites Only." I always wonder whose job it was to write such signs: was there a company that made its family's fortune on the production of them? On paper, wood, metal, stenciled with skill, carved into all colors of skin, scarring a nation.

They ordered coffee. I hope they ordered four white coffees, in the only moment that could have raised a mischievous smile in the midst of what was to be a very long day. The black waitress asked them to leave; trouble would only follow, they were assured. But trouble needs to be taunted and provoked at times. They were undeterred. The white manager demanded that they leave. They felt determined.

And they sat there, waiting.

They would have to wait for six months, but wait they did. And they were not on their own.

Justice attracts those desiring change; courage attracts those desiring to engage. Collaboration is the catalyst for change.

The next day the Greensboro Four multiplied and became twenty as more African Americans arrived for coffee. The next day, sixty men and women, African Americans and white Americans, squeezed onto the counter. Good collaboration is non-exclusionary.

By the fourth day, three hundred people arrived for coffee and justice from the tortured tapestry of the American racial landscape; their strand in the tapestry, instead of fraying in tension, began to be pulled tighter, creating unbreakable bonds of an awakening trust.

Resistance by those who wanted segregation, wanted control, was quick, fierce, and evil. The protestors were called names. They were spat on. Food was thrown at them. A fire was lit using one of their coats.

Still they waited.

Collaboration generates fortitude.

Sit-ins like these continued to spread across America. Collaboration for the common good is contagious.

Collaboration is the giving of one's self so that the sum is greater than the one. Without trust we cannot truly collaborate for change.

Woolworth's lost a lot of money. And then, Woolworth's reluctantly dropped its segregation policy. (It's incredible how justice is so closely attached to monetary gain.)

July 25, 1960 Coffee was served to all.
July 26, 1960 Coffee was served nationally to all.
July 2, 1964 President Johnson signed The Civil Rights Act.
August 6, 1965 The Voting Rights Act was enacted.

Affect one, affect many.

When we seek the common, we will find the change.

Trust needs collaboration. Trust is collaboration person-ified. In 1960, just being seen together in certain states could mean a home or church burned to the ground, even death. Without risking collaboration, these men and women would not be free. It's that acute. Without rees-tablishing trust between those fighting for freedom, this collaboration would never have brought this extraordinary freedom. It's that vital.

The last time I was in Washington, DC, I visited the Smith-sonian National Museum of American History. While there, I saw the four stools and counter where the Greensboro Four risked their personal lives for a public justice. As I reached across the velvet rope and touched those chairs, it reminded me that springtime has come—but that winters return. We cannot stop collaborating. When we stop col-laborating for justice, then we will freeze in time, and our souls will be touched by frostbite.

345 YEARS

It took from 1620 to 1965, 345 years, for African Americans to be free to get a coffee *almost* anywhere they wanted.

That's a long time to seek the peace and prosperity of a people, a city, and nation.

Togetherness, collaboration, is the fulcrum that brings peace to a people, a city, and a nation.

If we want to see any consistent, lasting change in our cities or our lives, we must collaborate, work together, and partner with others. We are one of many in need of the many; we are a tree amid a disharmonious ecosystem in need of a tune.

Collaboration is partnership, is an active community living in tune in pursuit of the common good for all. To collaborate is to work toward each other, to be family, to be community, to be church; and it takes work and commitment.

Become friends, and trust follows.

ARC

Precedent comes thick and fast when you're looking at collaboration. Just look around, just look at you and look at the Bible. It's soaked in collaboration.

From God's very breath blown into our lungs, to a shared rib in Genesis, through to Jeremiah seeking the peace and prosperity of the city, and right into the Gospels and Jesus incarnate being born to a courageous young girl. New moments of collaboration need to be lived today. These stories need to be lived and recorded; we need to keep writing the Bible with our lives.

But by far the best example of trust's restorative living was by the one who could've done it all by himself but chose not to.

211

LEFTOVERS

Let me imagine myself as another disciple, if only for a moment.

It seemed like any other day, which meant I had no idea where we were going and what could happen. I was a long way from home, the road to my new home. And if there was anything we knew, it was that we knew nothing.

Following Jesus would sometimes, to quote Tom Waits, be "like operating on a flamingo. You don't even know where the heart is, nothing. If you touch there, you know, the world will end. If you touch . . . here, I dunno, you may lose your hand. It has that kind of danger about it."[1]

Following this bearded Rabbi can be both deeply concerning and deeply exhilarating all at once.

What would it have been like to collaborate with the physical God there in the heat of the Middle East?

> Jesus: "Good morning! Did you catch anything for breakfast?"
>
> I answered with a soft yet resonating, "No."
>
> Jesus, the "fisher of men" who had grown up in a landlocked town, said far too confidently for my liking, "Throw the net off the right side of the boat and see what happens."
>
> It had been a slow day, and we were frustrated. We could do with a miracle. (I'm always amazed at how closely related frustration and miracles seem to be.) So we lifted our nets and threw

them to the east. In short, Jesus is a very handy guy to have around. Our nets were bursting with shimmering fish practically offering themselves to us; I'd never seen anything like it and never would again.

Jesus could've caught the fish by himself but chose to collaborate with us. He could've called the fish to obey, and they would've swam to shore, yet he got into the boat with us.

And our Rabbi didn't stop there. He did it again when needing to feed the crowd of thousands that gathered to listen, a community unprepared for a picnic, many times over five thousand. Jesus saw the need, and instead of just conjuring up the food we needed, or raining it down from the heavens like centuries ago, he found a young boy, and together they brought about a miracle. Jesus didn't ignore the needs of the people and just feed himself and those immediately around us. He fed everyone, even those who hadn't heard or were on the edges of the crowd or were distracted by the life swirling around them. We all ate.[2]

And then Jesus said, "Gather the leftovers so nothing is wasted" (John 6:12 *The Message*).

WASTED

In Jesus, nothing is wasted. What do we do with our leftovers? Even as a recession-filled planet, we cannot only give in times of plenty. We need to give in times of little.

Jesus letting us participate in these miracles sets a beautiful precedence for collaborative living.

Collaboration is self-less. Collaboration is presence, is present-tense.

THE UNWRAPPING

Returning to being a disciple from a first-person perspective:

> Greg aka disciple: Not long after this I could hear our Rabbi whispering. His voice had changed; it seemed to be tinged with sadness. He said to us, "Our friend Lazarus has fallen asleep. I'm going to wake him up."
>
> I couldn't understand why his cousin sleeping was bringing about such sadness; surely a bit of rest in the afternoon is what we all could use.
>
> Then the denarius dropped. Jesus, even now not tiring of explaining what was obvious to him yet discombobulating to us, said "Lazarus died. And I am glad for your sakes that I wasn't there. You're about to be given new grounds for believing. Now let's go to him."
>
> Quite simply, it was on. When that spark was in his eye, we knew that our belief was about to be stretched to its limits. (Something I had at first resisted but now embraced as an adventure I wanted to be on.)
>
> We could hear the grieving before we could see it. The family was distraught. A son, a brother, a

cousin was dead. But Jesus seemed more determined than ever as we walked to the tomb.

Not many things in my life have caused me to lose my breath, to freeze in my steps, to weep. But as I stood there close enough to see the rise and fall of Jesus' chest, I watched as he began to cry. A friend had been lost. We couldn't have known at that moment that it was temporary, but surely Jesus must have known; yet he took time to grieve, to share in our grief.

[Collaboration feels pain.]

What happened next seemed like a blur. Martha getting us the details that Lazarus had been dead for four days. A group of us rushing forward to move the stone away—not as simple as it seems. Then Jesus did the miraculous speaking, "Lazarus, come out!" And he came out, a cadaver, wrapped from head to toe, and with a kerchief over his face."

At times when following Jesus, OK pretty much all of the time, I had to question the sanity of my Rabbi and my own sanity; now he was shouting at corpses. And the corpse obeyed. His friend recognized his voice from the tomb.

I stood stunned. And then Lazarus started walking toward us, fully wrapped.

Did Jesus rush forward and revel in the glory moment—it was fully of his own doing—of the unveiling, the reveal, the unwrapping? No. He said to us, "Go and unwrap him, take off his death clothes for he is now alive."

This is Jesus letting us participate in the miracle, in the unwrapping of Lazarus. Jesus could've done this all by himself but chose to work with us.[3]

SOMETHING

Jesus sets a wonderful precedence for collaborative living.

Collaboration is not just a "Jesus" thing but an "us" thing.

Collaboration between God and humanity is beauty.

NOTHING

Jesus said, "I can of mine own self do nothing: as I hear, I judge: and my judgment is just; because I seek not mine own will, but the will of the Father which hath sent me" (John 5:30 KJV).

Trust and collaboration exemplified.

Collaboration is the very nature of God.

We are created to collaborate.

EGO

Why all these stories? Well, if you don't feel like you can change a nation . . . first, you're wrong, by God you can; but begin by changing that which surrounds you. Collaborating with God and others for others.

There is no ego in collaboration.
Collaboration between God and humanity is beautiful.
Collaboration means desiring the best for one another.
Collaboration means intentional living.

In this individualistic society and in our individualistic churches, it has become so easy to forget that life is meant to be a symphony of collaboration.

God invites us into collaboration. No more hiding ourselves away from the cities of Babylon or Dublin, London or Sydney, New York or Shanghai.

We cannot ignore the issues of the city from an ivory tower with a badge of entitlement saying, "Do you not know who I am? I'm am Israelite, I'm an Anglican, I'm a Catholic, I'm a Christian—I don't belong here—I'm so much better."

A senior member of the Irish government, Pat Rabbitte, said it was a "retro grade step to ask the church for moral advice."[4] Sadly, he makes good sense because we as a faith-based community and church have become turned toward power, gain, and reputation—and not turned toward one another.

Our voices are hoarse and will be lost and relegated to the gutters of history if we choose as a church, as a people of God, not to collaborate with others or different churches— as trust must be forged in unity. These parts of the body— the church—that are created to reach out and embrace will atrophy. In fact, they already are. But the erosion of hope must be halted.

When we choose to actively collaborate, a life, a city, a culture, a nation will change beyond recall.

True, honest, and humble faith, which is a by-product of good community and a good church, is real-time evidence of collaboration with everyone.

In Jesus, all are welcome; and if you don't believe it, then go out and tear down your welcome signs on the front lawns of your churches and make a bonfire. Church should be the uncaged, unsolicited, unrestricted, indiscriminating, overused, uncontrollable, beautiful, trusted, raw embrace of Jesus, for all. Church is collaboration.

FLASH POWDER

Jacob Riis grew up in a poor family of fifteen in Ribe, Denmark in the mid-1800s. His family had adapted to living in the shadow of the city, in the shadow of poverty. In 1870 he took a transatlantic steamship, with a pocket full of donated cash, and landed in New York with the hope of a new life.

This was (and still is) a time where the poor are hidden, thus unknown, out of sight and most definitely out of mind. But as Jacob wandered the streets getting to know his city, he began to find those without, those living in poverty in the shadows, gutters, alleyways, basements, and dark corners of the city. He was determined that history would not repeat itself, that the poor wouldn't struggle in a hidden poverty as he had.

Having secured a job at the *New York Evening Sun* as a photojournalist, Jacob began to document *How the Other Half Lives*,[5] yet the impact was mute—his photos were not turning out, there was nothing to illuminate the dark spaces inhabited by those most in need.

Then flash powder was invented. Jacob didn't hesitate. Light was coming to the hidden slums of New York City. Jacob quickly saw for himself what he knew instinctively: it's harder to ignore what we can see.

From a seemingly simple flash powder, the poor finally had faces.

For the first time in American history, change came in a radical way to the poor because someone chose to combine his passion for justice with the innovation of the day, a powerful collaboration.[6]

If we choose to courageously engage in the lives we lead, then we will effect change locally and even globally. There is plenty of precedent. Will we become part of these revolutions, even creating new ones?

When we turn toward one another, when we leverage our lives, when we intentionally pursue reestablishing trust, we will see lasting change in our own lives and in the lives we connect with; and those in power will pay attention.

Our shared stories can challenge and shake up belief systems. Rattled subcultures can create prophets—but be aware: we can also stone them. Still, we need to be more concerned with saving lives than saving our reputations, just as the Greensboro Four, Jacob Riis, and Jesus did. We have a cultural mandate to be restorers of trust.

Life is about embracing that which you were created for and discovering the shape of that which was, which is, and which will come. It's about demystifying innovation and initiation and mission. Every good idea begins with feeling or seeing a need and connecting with all that surrounds you.

Seth Godin said, "The essence of being human is initiating."[7] Whenever we actively choose to initiate and to give ourselves away, we create life; where we are indifferent, atrophy prevails. We start by following our passions and meeting people along that road. We start by looking for the need that surrounds us and entering into it.

We are the active daily restorers of trust between God and us, between us and us, in the guidance of the Holy Spirit. God could have just renewed all for all, but instead, God's choice was to collaborate in the renewing of our families and cities with us.

This life is not about having a bigger extension, a better job, or getting it right just to look right. This isn't about control; it's about listening to the Antons who convert us, about forgiving the absent fathers, about doing the art that causes us to transform our hearts and our streets. This life of faith is about doing the hard work of restoring trust.

Trust connects, creates, and collaborates.
Trust restores.
Trust heals.
You are created to restore trust.

I WANT. WE WANT?

I want to be a people and a church that restores trust in God.
I want to be a people and a church that restores trust in people.
I want the presence of peace to no longer be eroded in the tides of entitlement.
I want our lighthouses reignited.

I want us to find our voices again.

I want to re-imagine.

I want to listen more.

I'm tired of faking it. I want to be real.

I want to be a person and leader who lives in waking dreams.

I want to risk more.

I want relationship over opportunity and people over productivity and profit.

I want to celebrate your success.

I want to remember that all of this jostling for supremacy ends in an embrace.

I want to stop hesitating.

I want to be more than a cliché or groupie of the status quo.

I want to be spontaneous in generosity and lavish in encouragement.

I want a life that is absent of negative competition and comparison.

I want to love better.

I want to forgive quicker.

I want to be accused and found guilty of continuous "indiscriminate acts of kindness."[8]

I want to love in a way that empties myself for others.

I want a love that participates in another's pain and finds a way through it, together.

I no longer want to call it mission. I want to call it living.

I no longer want to call it worship. I want to call it being.

I want a love that seeks the common and finds the change.

I want a love that grasps the winter and wrings out the springtime.

I want to be in the Greensboro Four.

I want to be Jacob Riis.

I want to be me, broken and all.

I want to have parties in alleyways.

I want to climb mountains and have community picnics.

I want to be fully present.

I want "open arms for broken hearts."[9]

I want to collaborate with you.

I want this with you.

Do you?

Notes

INTRODUCTION

1. For more, see my TEDx Talk "Trust Your Scars" from Belfast's Cathedral Quarter, www.youtube.com/watch?v=_ADH11GTDGg.

1. TRUST AND FORGIVENESS: THE ADDICT, THE ARTIST, THE FATHER, AND HIS SON

1. Guy Edward John Garvey et al., "Ribcage," from the album *Cast of Thousands* by Elbow (New York: Warner Music Group, 2003).

2. Shane Claiborne, "Beating AK47s into Shovels," *Huffington Post* (August 15, 2013), www.huffingtonpost.com/shane-claiborne/beating-ak47s-into-shovels_b_3762948.html.

3. See "Tony Campolo's story of a gay son," www.youtube.com/watch?v=gWYtkn_8D-g.

4. Brian McClaren, "Is God Violent?" *Sojourners* (January 2011), http://sojo.net/magazine/2011/01/god-violent.

2. TRUST AND SEPARATION: THE EMBRACE OF "NOTHINGS"

1. Harry Nilsson, "One (Is the Loneliest Number)," rights administered by Warner-Tamerlane Music Corp.

2. Damien Rice, "Trusty and True," Warner/Chappell Music Publishing Ltd., 2014.

3. Dan Robins, *Perfect Love Too Good to Be True?* (Lulu Printing, 2012), 44. This quotation is often misattributed to Brennan Manning from his book with John Blase, *All Is*

Grace: A Ragamuffin Memoir (Colorado Springs: David C. Cook, 2011).

4. Guy Edward John Garvey et al., "Open Arms," from the album *Build a Rocket Boys!* by Elbow (London: Polydor, 2011).

3. TRUST AND PRESENCE: STRANGLING MY INNER JESUS

1. Brian Jones, *Jim Henson: The Biography* (New York: Ballantine, 2013).
2. Author's narrative based on Matthew 4:18-20.
3. Author's narrative based on Luke 5:1-10.
4. Author's narrative based on John 13:7-9.
5. Author's narrative based on Matthew 14:28-30.
6. Author's narrative based on John 18:10.
7. Author's narrative based on John 18:16-27 and Luke 22:45-46.

4. TRUST AND FEAR: THE DAY EVERYTHING CHANGED

1. Name changed on request.

5. TRUST AND POSTURE: LIVING WITH CHANGE

1. Foy Vance, "Gabriel and the Vagabond" (Glassnote Records, 2006), www.foyvance.com.
2. Raymond J. Mauer, *Duck and Cover*, archival film, directed by Anthony Rizzo (New York: NBC Universal, 1951).

6. TRUST AND RESTORATION: THE SHATTERING OF MISREPRESENTATION

1. Foy Vance, "Doesn't Take a Whole Day to Recognize Sunshine" (Triple R, 2007).
2. C. S. Lewis, *The Silver Chair* (New York: Collier, 1970).

7. TRUST AND FAITHFULNESS: WHO ME?

1. Reverend Archie Coates, Vicar at St. Peter's, Brighton, spoken live at Windsor Castle.
2. Scot McKnight, *The Real Mary: Why Evangelical Christians Can Embrace the Mother of Jesus* (Brewster, MA: Paraclete, 2007), 36.

8. TRUST AND FREEDOM: I CAN SEE CLEARLY NOW

1. Richard J. Mouw, *Abraham Kuyper: A Short and Personal Introduction* (Grand Rapids, MI: Eerdmans, 2011), 41.

2. Mouw, *Abraham Kuyper*, 58.

3. Mouw, *Abraham Kuyper*, 23, 41.

4. Based on the quote, "The assumption of spirituality is that always God is doing something before I know it. So the task is not to get God to do something I think needs to be done, but to become aware of what God is doing so that I can respond to it and participate and take delight in it." In Eugene H. Peterson, *The Contemplative Pastor: Returning to the Art of Spiritual Direction* (Grand Rapids: Eerdmans, 1989), 4.

5. I first read this in Mouw's *Abraham Kuyper*. I have since seen it credited to hundreds of other people.

6. James D. Bratt, ed., *Abraham Kuyper: A Centennial Reader* (Grand Rapids, MI: Eerdmans, 1998), 488.

7. John Maeda, *The Laws of Simplicity: Design, Technology, Business, Life* (Cambridge, MA: MIT Press, 2006), 19.

8. Maeda, *Laws of Simplicity*, 21.

9. Dean Nelson, *God Hides in Plain Sight: How to See the Sacred in a Chaotic World* (Grand Rapids: Brazos, 2009).

10. Van Gogh was the first artist I think I actually got. The book *Lust for Life: A Novel Based on the Life of Vincent Van Gogh* by Irving Stone contributed the most to my growing understanding (New York: Pocket Books, 1963).

11. I'm continually inspired by Banksy, the United Kingdom–based graffiti artist, political activist, film director, and painter. I actively seek out his work in any city he has been.

12. A cultural prophet, Tommy Tiernan is a controversial, hilarious, and insightful Irish comedian, actor, and writer.

9. TRUST AND BEING: WE, THE CHURCH

1. This section originally appeared in Greg Fromholz, "'Piece' Be with You," pages 64–71 in Jennifer Grant and Cathleen Falsani, *Disquiet Time: Rants and Reflections on*

the Good Book by the Skeptical, the Faithful, and a Few Scoundrels (New York: Jericho, 2014).

2. Cathal McNaughtan, "Fake Shop Fronts Hide N.Ireland Economic Woes Before G8," June 3, 2013, www.reuters .com/article/2013/06/03/us-irish-g8-fakeshops-idUS-BRE95210520130603.

3. Dan Keenan, "Recession Out of the Picture as Fermanagh Puts on Brave Face for G8 Leaders," May 29, 2013, www.irishtimes.com/news/recession-out-of-the-picture-as -fermanagh-puts-on-a-brave-face-for-g8-leaders-1.1409112.

4. Simon Sinek, "How Great Leaders Inspire Action," Ted Talk, http://www.ted.com/talks/simon_sinek_how_great_ leaders_inspire_action. Sinek is an ethnographer and leadership expert, described as "a visionary thinker with a rare intellect." www.startwithwhy.com.

5. Cameron is a self-described "dreamer, planner, doer, provoker, shaper, initiator, manager, communicator, deliverer." "I don't really fit in one category. I kind of like them all."

6. Roy Kerr, Freelance Hellraiser DJ (Sony/BMG, 2006).

10. TRUST AND PEACE: THE ABNORMALITY OF BEAUTY

1. This section originally appeared in Greg Fromholz, "'Piece' Be with You," pages 64–71 in Jennifer Grant and Cathleen Falsani, *Disquiet Time: Rants and Reflections on the Good Book by the Skeptical, the Faithful, and a Few Scoundrels* (New York: Jericho, 2014).

2. Alex Gibney and Hunter S. Thompson, *Gonzo: The Life and Work of Dr. Hunter S. Thompson*, directed by Alex Gibney (Magnolia Home Entertainment, 2008).

3. Fromholz, "'Piece' Be with You."

4. Fromholz, "'Piece' Be with You."

5. Fromholz, "'Piece' Be with You."

6. Fromholz, "'Piece' Be with You."

11. TRUST AND HOPE: EMBRACING OUR TRUE SELVES

1. Graham Kendrick, "The Servant King" (Thankyou Music, 1983).

2. Zoe Mintz, "St. Boniface Church in San Francisco Lets

Homeless People Sleep in Pews," *Huffington Post*, Jan. 31, 2013, www.huffingtonpost.com/2013/01/31/st-boniface -church-san-francisco_n_2592275.html.
3. Keith Gordon Green, "Asleep in the Light," *No Compromise* (Universal Music, 1978).
4. Edward James Milton Dwane et al., "Awake My Soul," from the album *Sigh No More* by Mumford and Sons (Universal Music, 2009).

12. TRUST AND SCARS: A LIFE OF BROKEN RESTORATION
1. Author's narrative based on John 20:19-31.
2. Ray Bradbury, "All Summer in a Day," *The Magazine of Fantasy and Science Fiction* (1954).
3. Author's narrative based on John 20:19-31.
4. Leonard Cohen, Theresa Christina Calonge de Sa Mattos, "Hallelujah" (Bad Monk Publishing, Sony/ATV Songs LLC).
5. Henri J. M. Nouwen, *The Wounded Healer: Ministry in Contemporary Society* (Colorado Springs: Image, 1979).

13. TRUST AND HONOR: THE RADICAL SOLIDARITY OF SERVICE
1. Gene Edwards, *The Tale of Three Kings: A Study in Brokenness* (Carol Stream, IL: Tyndale, 1992).

14. TRUST AND HOME: THE SOUND OF CRASHING TABLES IN SACRED SPACES
1. Greg Fromholz, "Evangelical in a Box," video, *Sojourners*, "God's Politics" with Cathleen Falsani (Oct. 18, 2011).
2. Walter Brueggemann, *The Prophetic Imagination* (Minneapolis: Augsburg Fortress, 2001), 4.

15. TRUST AND LIVING: ALL OUR BEAUTIFUL CASTLES
1. Henri J. M. Nouwen, *Out of Solitude: Three Meditations on the Christian Life* (Notre Dame, IN: Ave Maria Press, 2008), 47, 26. Authors note: buy this book, go now . . . put mine down and read *Out of Solitude*.
2. Cameron Crowe, *Jerry Maguire* (TriStar Pictures, 1996).
3. Billy Graham, "Is There an Answer?" a speech to the

Empire Club of Canada (Oct. 6, 1955), http://speeches
.empireclub.org/60975/data?n=21.

4. Mahatma Gandhi, *An Autobiography: The Story of My Experiments with Truth* (Boston: Beacon, 1993), 68.

5. Adam Clayton et al., "Every Breaking Wave," from the album *Songs of Innocence* by U2 (Universal Music Publishing Group, 2014).

16. TRUST AND COLLABORATION: SEEK THE COMMON

1. From "Tom Waits Meets Jim Jarmusch," Straight No Chaser (Spring 1993), http://jimjarmusch.tripod.com/snc93.html.

2. Author's narrative based on John 21:5.

3. Author's narrative based on John 11:1-44.

4. Raidió Teilifís Éireann (August 27, 2012).

5. Jacob Riis, *How the Other Half Lives: Studies among the Tenements of New York* (New York: Charles Scribner's Sons, 1890).

6. Irish singer-songwriter, author, actor, and political activist Bob Geldof used television in a similar way with Live Aid, the biggest benefit concert in history; he is also the adviser to the ONE Campaign.

7. Seth Godin, publisher, The Domino Project, 1st ed. (March 1, 2011).

8. "Indiscriminate Acts of Kindness" is the profound song and parable by Foy Vance (Wurdamouth Records, 2006).

9. Guy Edward John Garvey et al., "Open Arms" from the album *Build a Rocket Boys!* by Elbow (London: Polydor, 2011).